About Robert Dolling

Father Robert Dolling was born in Magheralin, Northern Ireland in 1851. Educated at Harrow School and Cambridge University, he was ordained in 1883 to a curacy in Corscombe, Dorset and headed St Martin's Mission to the poor in Stepney. From here he moved in 1885 to Saint Agatha's, Landport, Portsmouth.

He was recognised in his lifetime both as a tireless devotee to the most needy and as an Evangelical preacher with a reputation for speaking his mind. He was an Anglo-Catholic revivalist, which alongside his forthright views drew criticism from some parts of the Church of England.

His primary concern, however, was his flock. Drawn from the lowest reaches of society, they also became his friends. His energy and belief in the people he served made his message infectious, as this book documenting his mission to Portsmouth from 1885-1895 reveals.

About the editor

Matt Wingett was born in Portsmouth and has a fascination with the city.

He is a writer of fiction, history and tv drama. He has written several fiction stories based around Portsmouth, a study of Sir Arthur Conan Doyle's spiritualism and has written episodes of ITV's *The Bill* as well as stage plays.

Also by Matt Wingett

The Tourist
The Boiler Pool
The Tube Healer
Turn The Tides Gently
The Song of Miss Tolstoy
Conan Doyle and the Mysterious World of Light

He also contributed to and published:

Portsmouth Fairy Tales for Grown-Ups

TEN YEARS
IN A
PORTSMOUTH SLUM

R. Radclyffe Dolling

TEN YEARS
IN A
PORTSMOUTH SLUM

by

FATHER R R DOLLING

Edited by

MATT WINGETT

*Life Is Amazing
Heritage Series*

A Life Is Amazing Paperback
Ten Years In A Portsmouth Slum
First published in this edition 2015 by Life Is Amazing
ISBN: 978-0-9572413-4-3
First Thus Edition

CONTENTS

Editor's Introduction

The city of Portsmouth straddling the island of Portsea today is very different from the sprawl of towns and settlements to which the Reverend Robert Dolling was appointed in 1885.

Conway Street and the other rows of cramped housing that clustered around Dolling's crowning achievement, Saint Agatha's Church, Landport, were wrecked by a single explosion during World War II. Perhaps miraculously, the church of St Agatha's stands alone, surrounded by roads leading elsewhere, a little island of the past not completely swept away by the German bombs or modern traffic schemes - though the latter managed what the Germans couldn't and sliced off one of its chapels.

Standing in the church today, it is intriguing to imagine the maze of narrow streets that once surrounded the basilica, a church that opened just a few short weeks before Father Dolling departed after a doctrinal dispute with his bishop, despite his indefatigable attention to his flock, and to the fundraising needed to build the church. It is humbling to consider the thousands of lives Dolling's energy touched and the battles he fought to improve people's lots. It is also peculiar today to consider the basilica devoid of a parish, the crowding slums that were so much the focus of his attention long erased.

The portion of Landport that was Dolling's sphere of influence was crammed under the high walls of Portsmouth dockyard and stretched out towards Commercial Road.

The presence of the dockyard perhaps accounts for the attitude to life of many who lived on Portsea Island.

In the 1880s, 10,000 men, skilled and unskilled, made a living in the yard fitting out and repairing the ships that were the lifeblood of the British Empire. Their lives were hard and the skills required of them had little to do with being civilised or Christian. For many the qualifications needed were to be strong, to be able to strike a rivet accurately, to work hard and report for work not too much the worse for wear from excesses in pubs, alehouses, brothels, cockpits or any other of the previous night's places of entertainment.

Alongside the workers in the dockyard were the sailors. Men who had often been at sea for years on end, were battle-hardened and used to drinking to excess in the seedy backstreets of teeming Imperial ports the world over. Landport was one more such place.

The town of Portsmouth herself lay off to the south and west. Ostensibly genteel along its High Street, Portsmouth contained massive barracks where soldiers were penned, awaiting an insurrection or a war to call them to their duty.

With so many rootless men, and with an extraordinarily high number of watering holes around the town, it is little surprise that numerous prostitutes walked the streets looking for trade, or ran their businesses from more or less discreet "bad houses" in the airless recesses and narrow lanes of Landport, Portsea and Portsmouth.

The back streets of Portsmouth were slums. King's Bench Alley, Portsea, was only 2 feet 7 inches wide at its narrowest point, and never broader than 4 feet. Squeeze Gut Alley in Portsmouth had a name that told you all you needed to know about its size. The houses in Landport were similarly sardined. A toilet in a back yard might be shared between several families and running water was drawn from a communal pump.

Families were stacked close by and, as Dolling himself notes, were prone to a clannishness that meant people in one street wouldn't speak with those from the next.

With little need for education, since the dockyard would supply the work, existence was harsh and physical. The children playing on the streets moved among sailors, soldiers vagabonds, prostitutes, tramps and the workless at the very bottom of Victorian society.

Missing were what Father Dolling considered to be the elevating influences of religion, simple social interaction and community-building.

This was the challenge that met him in 1885.

Dolling was the son of a wealthy landowner in Northern Ireland,

English-educated, with a strong feeling for the presence of God in man. He was a simplistic theologian and a natural champion of common people.

Dolling's approach to the slums of Portsmouth suited his personality and that of the town. He was extremely active and soon realised that the children of these tough families would not want their religious lessons over-egged. It was more useful to the people around him if he give them the things missing from their lives - an opportunity for neighbours from different streets to socialise under one roof, the chance for young men and women to bring some gentleness to their courtships, the opening of a gymnasium, public baths, almshouses and a grand church - and the closing of the brothels.

He overcame the higher classes' prejudices against the poor, reformed those fallen into vice and challenged vested interests as he served his parish. He overcame, too, the practicalities of teaching his flock to live a more orderly life, not least the protests of mothers who complained their children's clothes were worn through by kneeling to pray.

All the while, Dolling firmly took their side, and actively so. His preferences were against the intellectual, and in favour of the practical. His attitude to the poor and the uneducated is stated clearly in a few words that reveal the stance he took to Portsmouth:

"For ten long years, day and night, there were lessons for me to learn, if I only had the grace and modesty to learn them. Even in that in which men might know more, knowledge, they are but as babes and sucklings in the presence of those whom they condescend to teach, that is, if knowledge means the knowing of things likely to be useful to the knower and to the community. In speech, too, how much we have to learn; how terse and in what few words do our dear people express themselves, while the man who wants to harangue them wraps round with innumerable words, which darken all counsels and prevent all understanding, the thought that the slum lad expresses in three or four words to the point. And as to manners, every single man in my home was a gentleman, that is, if thinking

*for others and treating them with forbearance and
tenderness and love, and striving to make them feel at home
and at ease, means being gentlemen. The roughest, rudest,
most ignorant lad, after a month's residence, has obtained
these graces."*

This book is Dolling's account of his time in Portsmouth. It is rich
with the flavour of the Anglo-Catholic church in the 19th Century -
and with something else besides. It gives an insight into the life of the
town, the different strata of society and the characters who lived
here.

It reveals the gulf between the classes, sometimes with humour –
as with Bishop Thorold's astonishment upon being told that the two
charming men he had sat next to during a dinner in Landport were
accomplished thieves, or the way in which Dolling took his flock out
for visits to amazed and aghast wealthy benefactors in the country in
an effort to infuse them with the finer points of civilization.

Throughout, Dolling reveals the emotional satisfaction he drew
from crafting a society that didn't only see its members as economic
entities, but as people who had the right to enjoy themselves in
activities other than drinking and gambling, He shows how providing
amenities for them had a positive effect on the people's humanity –
something those in power of late appear to have forgotten.

He also reveals the humour of life as a priest in Portsmouth, the
highs and the lows. The children who wrecked the gymnasium just
because they could, the begging priest whom Dolling took by the
scruff of the neck and threw out of his house, the visiting Member of
Parliament, the guardsman and clergymen staying with him over
Christmas whom he put on a ration of cheese and bread with the rest
of the household as punishment for whomever wrecked Blind Willie's
hat.

In his account of the vibrant, rich life of Portsmouth there is
darkness, light, despair and hope.

In all, there is much to recommend the Reverend Robert Dolling's
book, and much to marvel at.

Enjoy!

Matt Wingett, Southsea, Portsmouth, 2015

AUTHOR'S DEDICATION.

TO
MY SISTERS, ELISE AND GERALDINE
TO
LINA BLAIR, FLORENCE WELLS
AND
MATILDA ROWAN
WHO FOR THE SAKE OF GOD BORE WITH ME
FOR TEN YEARS
IN ALL GRATITUDE I DEDICATE THIS LITTLE BOOK
WHICH IS VIRTUALLY
AN ACCOUNT OF THEIR WORK.

PREFACE

To those who know the work of the Winchester College Mission I need offer no explanation why this little book is written, and no apology for the scrappy and imperfect manner of the writing. But if it falls into the hands of those who do not know us, I would plead as an excuse for its many imperfections, that it was written in the odd moments seized out of a very busy Lent, in which I was preaching ten courses of sermons a week, striving to collect money to pay off the debt of £3090, incurred on the Mission, for which I am responsible. I pray that these readers will discover that Mission work like ours, for which so many great cities in England are crying out, is not only the easiest of all religious work to do, but is far the most satisfying in the doing; and I desire to create a great sympathy for the poor folk at S. Agatha's who were compelled, as they were crossing the stream from an old church into a new one - the most critical moment of their parochial existence - to swop horses, because a new commander discovered that the methods of their old one were not quite orthodox.

R. R. DOLLING.

48, Wetherby Mansions,

Earl's Court, S.W. Easter Day, 1896.

I.
My Appointment.

I FEAR the title of this little book is almost a libel; but, as the parent often looks upon the grown-up son as if he were still a child, so do my thoughts ever go back to the infancy of our work, and S. Agatha's is a slum district in my mind. Though we have largely lost the outward visible signs of slumdom, poverty, of course, remains - it always will - but utter hopelessness and callous depravity have, in a large measure, passed away, not merely from our people, but from our very streets.

We are a curious little island in this great town of Portsmouth. The Unicorn Road, leading to the Dockyard, the Edinburgh Road, leading to Portsea, and the Commercial Road - the main artery of all the traffic of the town - form a kind of irregular square, with the Dockyard wall as a base; and if it were not that Charlotte Street, which in happier days used to be called "Bloody Row," from the number of butchers' shops in it, and slaughter-houses behind it, is the thoroughfare which the Dockyard men mostly use in reaching their homes, we should be almost an unknown spot. This kind of isolation is one of the difficulties which the municipal authorities have had to face in making Portsmouth the great city they desire to see it.

Portsmouth is composed of four separate towns. When Portsmouth and Portsea - the former thronged with soldiers, the latter with sailors - High Street, Portsmouth, being a kind of parade ground; the Hard, Portsea, a kind of inland quarter-deck - burst their bonds, and the moats were removed, they developed, on the one hand, into Southsea, inhabited mostly by half-pay officers, with many hotels and lodging-houses, and, in the other direction, into Landport and Kingston, inhabited mostly by artisans in the Dockyard. This quadruple town, with its different, and often conflicting, interests, with an extraordinarily rapid increase of population, with its absence of wealthy people, and with hardly any manufactories, has been a very difficult mass out of which to create a really united city; and yet the progress which has been made even in my ten years has been very wonderful. Southsea has become a beautiful and fashionable watering-place; we have a splendid Town Hall and People's Park; the electric light has been most efficiently installed; the School Board has created through the town many magnificent schools; and when an attempt, which has been begun, is completed, of removing some of the slums which disgraced Portsmouth and Portsea, the town will become in some true sense worthy of its great historic interest.

All these changes have hardly affected our little district. The streets are, most of them, very narrow and quaint, named after great admirals and sea-battles, with old-world, red-tiled roofs, and interiors almost like the cabins of ships - many times I have stuck in a staircase, and could not go up or down till pulled from below - with the far-off scent of the sea coming over the mud of the harbour, and every now and then the boom of a cannon, or the shrill shriek of the siren; sailors everywhere, sometimes fighting, sometimes courting, nearly always laughing and good-humoured, except when afraid that they have broken their leave - our chief joy, alas! oftentimes our greatest danger. I remember well how, the first night I made acquaintance with it, their uniforms and rolling gait redeemed from its squalor and commonplace this poor little district, with its eleven hundred little houses and its fifty-two public-houses. Charlotte Street was, from end to end, an open fair; cheap-jacks screaming; laughing crowds round them, never seeming to buy; women, straggling under the weight of a baby, trying to get the Sunday dinner a little cheaper because things had begun to get stale; great louts of lads standing at the corners - you can guess from their faces the kind of stories they are telling; then some piece of horse-play, necessitating a sudden rush through the crowd, many a cuff and many a blow, but hardly any ill-nature; slatternly women creeping out of some little public-house. But why try and describe it to you? You have seen many such spots in any of our large towns. In my mind was but one single thought - "God has sent me to teach these people that they are His children, and that, therefore, they are priceless in His eyes."

I think if I had paid this visit before I accepted the Mission, I never should have accepted it. The shrill gaiety was a revelation to me of utter hopelessness, such as I had never imagined before. I was very seedy, too, at the time. I had left London soon after Bishop Jackson's death - the death of a bishop seems ever to be my note of warning. Dr. Fearon had heard very kind things about me from Bishop Walsham How, and I think some old Wykehamists at New College and Magdalen must have told him about me too. But I certainly was never more surprised in my life than when I got his letter asking me to go and see him. An interview with a Headmaster, the very idea of his study, filled me with alarm. Memories of Dr. Butler's study at Harrow came back with no pleasant suggestions. Yet I date from that interview with Dr. Fearon ten years of the happiest life that I can imagine possible for anyone. How large a part of that happiness Winchester has contributed, this little book will tell. I felt from that moment that, if the Mission was to be worthy of its name, it must achieve amongst Missions a place second to none. Even in that first visit, three facts about Winchester struck me - its simplicity, its unity, its solidity. These three notes we have tried to translate into Landport. It was three months after this visit that I first saw Winchester men at home. Yet looking back I seem to have stepped at once from Dr. Fearon's study into the great Hall of College, so entirely in my mind was Dr. Fearon's offer of the Mission finally ratified by the men. Dr. Linklater, with great kindness, came to introduce me to them. One of the dons said to me, as we went into the Hall, "Linklater has taken all our hearts by storm," and that was no more than the truth - I saw it in their faces, I heard it in their cheers. Is there any discordant note so full of harmony and music as the cheers of schoolboys? And in some true sense those cheers are still ringing in my ears; they have been my incentive in the hour of sloth, my rest in the hour of weariness, ever since.

I do not think I dreaded the interview with the Bishop at Farnham nearly so much as that with Dr. Fearon. I had known many Bishops, but no Headmaster before. And, curiously, Dr. Harold Browne revealed to me the very three notes I had discovered at Winchester - most simple, most balanced, most solid. I felt he had heard strange stories about me. Indeed, I think at first he was more nervous than I was. But when I saw the overwhelming weight which Portsmouth seemed to be to him, when he told me how it was always in his prayers and in his heart, and when, though he hoped I would not do anything foolish, he left me full liberty of operation, saying that his one hope, as far as we were concerned, was that the splendid work, which Dr. Linklater had begun, might be consolidated and perfected, I left Farnham Castle with a great increase of courage and hopefulness, though I had to pawn my watch to pay for a bed, as I could not get home that night. If for a moment during the interview I had wondered why a heart so occupied with his enormous diocese had such a large part of it sacred to Portsmouth, the work and energy of Sister Emma, the head of the Deaconesses, subsequently explained to me this interest. She has had more than any other single person to do with the bettering of Portsmouth. Its sins and sorrows had burned so deeply into her heart, that she could not fail to create in anyone, who saw her constantly, a reflection of her own feelings. The Bishop having placed her and her community there, was in constant communication with her. A Commission, too, had just reported to his Lordship on the state of the town. Its most prominent members were Mr. John Pares and Admiral Hornby, the former still a most earnest defender of all that makes for righteousness in Portsmouth; the latter, alas! called from the midst of his many labours, but who, as a sailor knowing every inch of Portsea, had influenced not only the Admiralty, but all thinking men with the thought that something needed doing in Portsmouth.

These two ordeals past, a worse one remained. I had to hear from Dr. Linklater's own lips the ideals he had created for the Landport Mission. He had sent me some of his reports; they were enough to frighten anyone from trying to follow in his footsteps. He had had efficient helpers; these I had yet to discover. He was a *persona grata* with the Naval and Military authorities; this, I was sure, I never would be. He had a tact in dealing with people almost unique, and a personal influence which remains in the hearts of many S. Agatha's people still, though he has hardly been in Landport for ten years, and a buoyancy and hopefulness which disappointment seemed to increase, and even illness could not abate. When I tried to square my

OLD SAINT AGATHA'S

memory of the Saturday night which I had seen in Charlotte Street with his ideals, no problem in mathematics ever seemed so impossible.

I had never had the pleasure of seeing him, but directly I arrived at the railway station I knew him. "I cannot talk to you here," he said; "let us get back into the train again, and go to Rowland's Castle. I don't want you to see Landport as it is; I want you to see it as I desire it to be."

There is an avenue of trees - you can see it from the train, just before you get into Rowland's Castle. I suppose that once it led up to some great mansion, but now it seems to stand alone, and it dominates the whole country.

"I want you to promise," he said, "that you will come here once a week; better still, take a walk over these downs for four or five miles; better still, sleep in the pure country air, if possible, once a week."

I believe if I had made time to keep this as a rule of my life, our work at Landport would have been far more successfully fulfilled. The plan of campaign - the best manner of working it out in detail - is not possible in the strife of the battle and the tumult of the conflict; this is what he wanted me to learn. One by one, as he talked them over, his ideals already seemed to have taken form - a great church with a staff of clergy, dignified services, efficient preaching, a centre of Catholic devotion, making its way through all the different strata of Portsmouth society; a free school for the children of the parish, a high school for those of a better class; social work of all kinds and descriptions, with one single intention, the drawing together into one Christian family all kinds and classes; real homes for soldiers and sailors, in which they might be equipped with that armour which alone could make them victorious in their hours of temptation; above all, to make Winchester rejoice, share, and understand every part of the work. And then, as we hurried back to Portsmouth, he said, "Now you will see what we have already achieved."

And so, from the ideal to the real, to S. Agatha's with its chancel screened off, its walls covered with religious pictures, all fresh and new, loving hands having painted Christian emblems all over it, goodnature and fun beaming from every face - for Dr. Linklater had gathered those connected with the church to meet me - with a joke for one, and a clout for another, we passed along, until we reached the centre of the room, and then - "Here is your new clergyman. What do you think of him?"

One of my chief causes of thankfulness to-day is that many of those in S. Agatha's that night are still Sunday School teachers, on the altar, and earnest communicants.

As I celebrated the Holy Communion the next morning, with the debris of the party still round me, though some attempt had been made to clear it away, I was lost in amazement at my own presumption in daring to undertake a work which seemed at that moment so impossible.

II.
My District

I DID not really begin my work till September 29th, 1885, but as Dr. Linklater wanted to go away, I came down to help on Sundays, and, therefore, I had the opportunity of learning something about the district before my work really began. A very wise priest once said to me, "Don't make plans for your parish, let your parish make plans for itself." These six weeks were invaluable, letting me hear the parish voices, and try to discover its plans. Two notes were always making themselves heard; one was the poverty, the other was the sin. And surely they explained each other; they were sinful as a rule, because they were poor. A man who falls from a height is wounded to death, every limb is shattered, every feature disfigured. He who slips on the pavement by a casual chance, pulls himself up, and goes on unhurt. Oh, most blessed truth! our falls in Portsmouth entailed no complete destruction of character, hardly any disfigurement at all. Boys stole, because stealing seemed to them the only method of living; men were drunken because their stomachs were empty, and the public-house was the only cheerful place of entertainment, the only home of good fellowship and kindliness; girls sinned, because their mothers had sinned before them, oftentimes their grandmothers too, unconscious of any shame in it, regarding it as a necessary circumstance of life, if they were to live at all. The soul unquickened, the body alone is depraved, and, therefore, the highest part is still capable of the most beautiful development. I wish I had any words in which I could put this thought quite plainly before you. It lies at the keynote of all missionary work, and it is what makes missionary work so full of hope.

My first Sunday afternoon, as I was walking in Chance Street, I saw, for the first time, a Landport dance. Two girls, their only clothing a pair of sailors' trousers each, and two sailor lads, their only clothing the girls' petticoats, were dancing a kind of breakdown up and down the street, all the neighbours looking on amused but unastonished, until one couple, the worse for drink, toppled over. I stepped forward to help them up, but my endeavour was evidently looked upon from a hostile point of view, for the parish voice was translated into a shower of stones, until the unfallen sailor cried out, "Don't touch the Holy Joe. He doesn't look such a bad sort." I could not stay to cement our friendship, for the bell was ringing for children's service, and, to my horror, I found that some of the children in going to church had witnessed the whole of this scene. They evidently looked upon it as quite a legitimate Sunday afternoon's entertainment. One little girl, of about eight, volunteered the name of the two dancing girls; she was a kind of little servant in the house, though she slept two or three doors off, and her only dread was that the return of a sailor, who had more rights in the house, might take place before the others had been got rid of.

You can imagine my feeling of hopelessness in conducting a service for children old in the knowledge, if not in the habits, of sin. Poor children, they had not been long accustomed to a church of their own; they had driven themselves away from the parish church by their behaviour. A neighbouring vicar, who kindly took them in for a little while, had left them in undivided enjoyment of his church, saying to Dr. Linklater, "I leave my church to you and your savage crew." My first attempt reached a climax when two boys calmly lighted their pipes and began to smoke. One remedy alone seemed possible - to seize them by the back of the neck, and run them out of church, knocking their heads together as hard as I could. Amazed at first into silence, their tongues recovered themselves before they reached the door, and the rest of the children listened, delighted, to vocabulary which I have seldom heard excelled. We had no sooner restored order than the mothers of the two lads put in an appearance. As wine is to water, so was the conversation of the mothers to their sons. I wish I could have closed the children's ears as quickly as I closed the service. But they listened with extreme delight, even following me in a kind of procession, headed by the two ladies, to my lodgings. The contrast between this, my first procession, and the last, which took place when my church was opened, is a true measure of the difference which ten years have made.

These two little episodes, which stand out so plainly in my memory, forced upon me the knowledge of our shameless sinfulness, and of our utter lawlessness and disobedience. But was it any wonder that it should be so? The wages of the majority of the people in regular employment were so small that they lived in continuous poverty; the larger part had no settled wages at all, many of them being hawkers, greengrocers with a capital of five shillings, window cleaners in a district where no one wanted their windows cleaned, old pensioners past work with a shilling to eighteenpence a day, sailors' wives with three or four children living upon £2 a month, and soldiers' wives married off the strength with no pay at all. One week's sickness of the bread-winners meant a fortnight's living upon the pawning of clothes and furniture, with nothing before them but the workhouse, and death sooner than that. Of course, there were many exceptions to this generalisation, but I am speaking of the parish as a whole. Then, temptation at almost every door, places where you were always welcome, even if you had no money, for there is always somebody to treat you; places where there are always the outward visible signs of rollicking goodnature, of mirth and jest; places where the craving of the empty stomach can be satisfied, where the crying wife and the hungry children may be forgotten; places where, it is only just to add, extraordinary kindness is often shown, and help given in the hour of direst need, for there is a good and kindly side even to the public house. Oh, that the bishops had the energy of the brewers! Oh, that the clergy had the persistency of the publicans! For what had the Church of England done for this district? Literally nothing. The enormous mother-parish of All Saints had its twenty-seven thousand parishioners, one church, one vicar, one curate. What even had Nonconformity done in its more recognised forms? One chapel, empty, minister and congregation having migrated to more favoured climes. But though the priest and Levite had passed by, the Good Samaritan had been represented by four little centres of earnest religious work, which have flourished during my whole ten years, and still are, thank God, working for Him in S. Agatha's district.

SOME OF OUR WORKERS

In one of these, the most ecclesiastical, a man, who worked six days a week in the Dockyard, laboured every night amongst the poor, and preached all day Sunday. The influence of this good Mr. Grigg will never be forgotten; many souls bless him in Paradise to-day. I shall never forget his funeral; it was the most touching sight I ever saw in Portsmouth. His example of honest labour, and of a life which proved the depth of his religious convictions, was beyond all price in the Dockyard. When you hear people talk glibly of orthodoxy, of dissent, of the exclusive rights and privileges of the Church, I pray you realize how many places would be virtually heathen, if the Church of England was the only representative of God in England. It is quite true that Nonconformity, in its more dignified congregations, fails, I think, largely in the slums; but there is a vast body of unattached Christians, or of laymen with their hearts aflame with the love of souls, with some kind of quasi-authority from more respectable chapels, preaching the Gospel literally without money and without price. Do not scoff at it, because it does not square with your own ideas. It is possible that it may be very faulty in itself. But the poor, tired, ignorant soul has no time to enter into questions like this, and the name of Jesus, when spoken by a believer, always sounds sweet in the ears of those who hear it. We cannot hope to build churches in every new district, we cannot hope to endow parishes, we cannot hope to pay adequate incomes to University-educated men. But we are the Church of England: we are responsible for the souls of every single man, woman, and child. Why cannot we create an enthusiasm amongst working men, toiling six days in the week, to give the seventh for the conversion of souls? The instrument may not be polished, may not be fitted to speak soft words politely, to enunciate theological truths exactly. What does it matter? What does it matter? We have as good stuff in the Church of England as in any other religious body. We have as much love for souls, as much self-denial, amongst our people. What hinders it? What represses it? The freehold, and the jealousy of the clergy, the fearfulness of the bishops to make any venture for faith, to allow any work to be undertaken that is not safe, that is not respectable.

Amid, then, all the sin, poverty, and squalor of S. Agatha's district - not a new district, remember, which increase of population had created, but a district of which every house had been built a hundred years ago - the only witness for God, until Dr. Linklater came, except an endeavour which Mr. Shute, the vicar of S. Michael's, had made some few years before, had been the devotion and love of a few poor Nonconformists,

I think the lesson, which I chiefly learned from the parish voice, was that Jesus alone could change the characters of men, and that no reformation can take place without this change of character. I realized that our Lord, if He had been in my place, would have fed the hungry, clothed the naked, healed the sick, visited those in prison; above all, removed stumbling-blocks from the ways of little children. I knew that we must try and do the same. I knew that their poverty, their nakedness, their ignorance, their punishments, were their strongest appeal; that He Himself was practically suffering in every one of them; that He was lying at our door full of sores, that we might share the wonderful privilege of healing Him. But I learned something more than this, that even if I was able to ameliorate all these circumstances, to make them all healthy, educated, able to earn a good day's wages, I might indeed have made it easier to do the one thing needful; but that one thing would still be undone until they had discovered that they, by His grace, must cure the ills of the soul, must clothe the nakedness of the spirit, that no one could set them free from sin save themselves, and that by His grace. In other words, strive as hard as ever you might to improve environment, to conquer even heredity, unless you have changed character, man is bound to remain helpless, though his helplessness may consist in a new weakness.

III.
Our Gymnasium

I HAVE said that we came without plans. And yet at every step, as we needed it, the Providence of God rendered possible the fulfilment of the plan, which the voice of the parish suggested. Bishop Harold Browne had evinced considerable nervousness, when I said I should bring my sisters down to Landport. He suggested that their dress might frighten the people. I said I hoped it would not. He intimated other difficulties. But his face brightened up considerably, when I told him that they were fleshly and not religious sisters, whom I hoped to bring with me. The first voice of the parish said, "We want Christian women." God put it into the heart of three of my sisters, and of two dear friends, who lived with them, to say, "We want to go into every house in Landport, to know every woman, every girl, every child."

Then another voice spoke, not always heard by the clergy, though it cries out louder to-day than it ever did before, the voice of the hard-headed artisan, the voice of the young man who is just beginning to face intellectual struggle, a voice for which the Free Library and the Press are largely responsible. That voice said, "We want an intellectual thinker, who can put deep profound truths into simple words, who can answer difficulties without suggesting others, who knows something of that agony of doubt without which no soul reaches the summit of faith, and has pity and compassion for it." And God put it into the heart of Charles Osborne to say, "I want to consecrate all my intellect, all my knowledge, to the lessening of doubts, to the building up of the faith, amongst the working-men in Landport."

And yet there was a need of a link between the past and the present, of someone to give me true advice about Sunday School

Teachers, District Visitors, Communicants, Choir, all those things which my predecessor had created; and God put it into the heart of Gordon Wickham, who had worked two years with Dr. Linklater, to say, "Though it will be very difficult to stay on under a new *régime*, yet for the sake of the past, for love of the people, for hope of the future, I stay."

God had given us the workers; would He also give us the places to live in? I was then in lodgings over a girls' school in the Commercial Road. It was not at all a desirable plan. The woman who did for me was utterly inadequate. I remember discovering in one Saturday's dinner the remains of Friday's, for our vegetables were garnished with fish-bones. The lodging, too, was out of the district. Then I took a house in Spring Street, where there was a heavy rent to pay, a ginger-beer factory on one side, a public-house on the other. The difficulty of housing ourselves was not the only house difficulty we had to face. Dr. Linklater had started a Men's Club, three Boys' Clubs, and a Girls' Club. The rent of premises to contain these cost over £120 a year, the buildings were very unsuited to the purpose, and there was a tremendous waste of energy in the management of them. I believed that no good daily example could be set until a clergy house could be provided, which would be our people's house as well as our own, and no real disciplinary or recreative work could be done in clubs until we had proper accommodation. S. Agatha's church, with the chancel screened off, had been used, as I knew from my own experience on my first introduction to the people, for entertainments of all kinds, teas, theatricals, even dances; but I made up my mind from the first that this should never happen again. Reverence is a very difficult virtue, and I am quite sure that the remembrance of the entertainments oftentimes marred the devotion at religious service. I remember once scolding a boy for laughing in church, and he said, "I could not help it, I was thinking of Mr. D---- singing 'Johnny Sands.'" The only premises at my disposal besides the church were a row of houses, which had been purchased as a site for the new church. Two standing in Conway Street were less picturesque, but rather more commodious than the rest, slate roofs, no red tiles. I thought these could be turned into a Mission House. Pulling down the middle partitions, lowering the floors of the downstairs rooms, so as to make

two good sitting-rooms below, and joining the houses by an outside
balcony, we had our parsonage; not just, perhaps, your idea of a
parsonage, but the door open all day, no mat to remind you that your
boots were dirty, no carpets, and the plainest furniture, plenty of
space in the dining-room to feed all comers, just room enough in the
kitchen to cook the food; upstairs four bedrooms to begin our home.

I hope I have never been jealous of any Christian work done in my
parish, but I must confess that there is something peculiarly
irritating in the music of the Salvation Army drum, though I am not
sure whether the shrill voice of the Salvation Army lass is not worse. I
remember one night they out-voiced me altogether, though I was
inside and they outside S. Agatha's. By way of consolation someone
said to me, "We shall have them always with us now, for they are just
going to buy the Baptist Chapel in Clarence Street." I registered a vow
that they never would. Why could I not buy the chapel in Clarence
Street? In many ways it was just suited for our purpose. It was a
splendid property. The chapel itself had a gallery all round, square
pews, three-decker pulpit, a font for immersions, and two dead
ministers buried in the middle. Next door was the caretaker's house,
which would just do for Mr. Osborne, and in the street behind,
Chance Street, an excellent Sunday School-room, and two cottages. It
cost me in all over £3000. I had not a penny of money, but it was so
obviously what the parish needed, that I knew we were bound to buy
it. I collected something like £1200 in a very few months, and the
bank kindly advanced me the balance to pay off the trustees. I was
fairly intoxicated at the purchase; I even communicated my
enthusiasm to others, so that at Winchester, where I was lecturing,
they realised my idea of a great social centre. Alas, when with
considerable pomp I ushered the four prefects, who were staying
with me that week, into the building, they, who very likely had never
seen a chapel before, said, "Now you have got it, what will you do
with it?" I suppose that at the best of times the chapel of a hundred
years ago never looked very picturesque, but this had been closed for
nearly two years, the grotesque pews were worm-eaten, the
ridiculous pulpit had an enormous Bible still upon the ledge, and,
with the stagnant water still in the font, I think we even realised the
bones of the ministers. I never felt so crestfallen. "At any rate, we can

kick down some of the pews." How delightful is the pleasure of destruction. One after another they were coming down, until prudence reminded me that they could be sold for something better than firewood.

Of course, there was the little difficulty at first of placing the old clubs in their new home. These little old clubs had many jealousies; one had driven out a member, after nearly breaking his head, because he would wear a collar, which they wanted to wrench off his neck, the collar being the outward visible sign of respectability; one was so ritualistic, that they would not allow anyone to join, who would not make the sign of the Cross; one so depraved, that losing all patience with the members who persisted in using the most disgusting language in the presence of the lady who managed them, I was compelled to chuck their leader downstairs, and almost broke his leg. Dear "Boss," how well I remember him, for so we called him, as he had a cast in his eye, though none in his temper, for he forgave me that very night. Two virtues were common to them all - utter lawlessness, supreme exclusiveness.

We furnished the chapel with all things necessary for a rough gymnasium, the gallery being used for games and bagatelle. The rules were the simplest - no gambling, no bad language, no losing of temper, no annoying anybody else. All through the ten years of use, these four rules have remained as the foundation of our management. All sorts and kinds of men have tried to manage that gymnasium, with varying success, the clergy, the lay-readers, Oxford men, officers in the Army and Navy. They have suffered all sorts of contumely and wrong. I have seen them skilfully lassoed, arms and legs bound, and lashed to the gymnasium ladder, or a noose run under their armpits, and hauled up to the ceiling. I have seen them spread-eagled upon the vaulting-horse, with a dance of savage Indians whooping round them. I have seen all the mattresses ripped up and picked to pieces, then strewn over the floor. I have seen the bagatelle-tables used as points of vantage, from which opposing forces sprang at each other. I have seen men playing upon the piano with their feet, and I have known, when no other mischief was possible, the fierce joy of tearing away the front of the piano, and strewing the broken hammers artistically on the floor. And yet there rises before me the vision of a use in that gymnasium, the chief centre of reformation in the parish, of lads who amidst all this disorder, for the disorder arose merely from episodes of high spirits or weak management, gained their first lessons of self-restraint, and bodily and even mental development; weak, sickly lads coming to us, illness not always the cause of their weakness, now healthy and strong; bad-tempered sullen brutes licked into shape, boys learning the priceless benefit of wholesome play, mean unambitious people quivering with the passion of desiring to achieve success. How often the lad, just needing the inch to become a soldier, has won it by continuous use of our ladders, how often the lad, needing an inch in chest measurement, has won it by the use of our dumb-bells, many a regiment, many a gallant ship, could testify to-day. How many it has won from the awful fascination of the public-house, from the vulgarity and worse of the sing-song room, from the delirium of gambling, from hideous forms of sins, impossible for those who desire to achieve a wholesome mind in a wholesome body! From all parts of the world, strong, healthy self-respecting men, bless and praise God for the old gymnasium in Clarence Street. Some years ago, when I was at Vienna, I was watching a troupe of acrobats in one of the beer-gardens. They had reached their final feat by forming themselves into a living ladder, when suddenly, in a kind of ecstasy, I heard the topmost boy exclaim, "Don't you see? there is the Father"; and before I knew where I was, three out of the five had precipitated themselves, and were clinging round me. There are scattered throughout the world to-day my brave army of gymnasium boys, but I believe they know that the Father's eye is still on them, and I know their love still compensates my heart for many of its sorrows. You say, "Mr. Dolling, were you not very imprudent in spending so much money on an object which was not religious? What fruit did it bring forth in your church? Did it pay ecclesiastically?" I can reckon in that sense no fruit. I do not believe that in that sense it paid. So often-times, when we hear of the great waste of time and energy spent on games at school and college, we are inclined to think it wasteful, sometimes to condemn it as being of the Philistine character. But anything that is graceful, and done with true skill and just precision, in itself ministers to the highest beauty; anything that tends to the

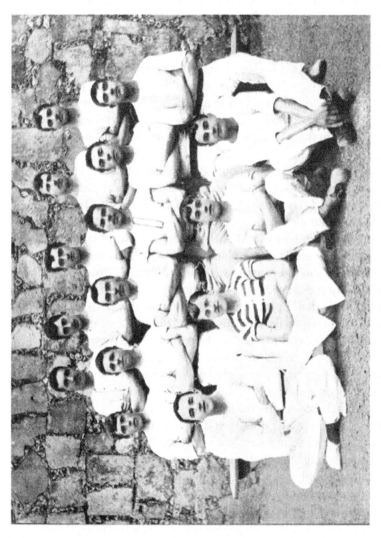

OUR GYMNASTS

perfecting of the body, to the sweating out of the evil humours of discontent; anything that cures sloth and gives an incentive to activity, ministers not only to the purifying of the body, but to the strengthening and increase of the soul. I have heard a mother say,"When my boy comes home, he can talk of nothing but games." Dear lady, if it is so, thank God; many boys talk of things evil and base and enervating.

The best effort that had been made under the old regime, and, I think, the manager who was most successful even in the gymnasium, was my old friend Charlie Claxon; and though stress of work and other reasons forced him to give up personal supervision, most of the old gymnasium members will remember him as a true and real friend.

One class of lad baffled all our allurements. Standing at the street corners all night, and most of the day, we got to know them by sight sooner than anybody else in the parish. In East London they had crowded into our club-rooms, and soon became amenable to order. I suppose one never learns that one's own plans always fail, and yet that God always has His own plan. Late one night I was sent for to go to the hospital. An old woman was slowly dying of burns; drink and a paraffin lamp the cause. I only knew her by sight, and she did not seem to listen when I prayed; but, as I stooped down, to try and catch any word she might say, she whispered, "He didn't do it," and then nodded with her head to a boy in the corner of the room. In five minutes she was dead.

When I had got the son quieted down in my own house, I found that he had come suddenly home, found her under the influence of drink, and in some scuffle the lamp had been upset.

Dear Dan, there was not much difficulty afterwards in getting hold of him, but I soon found it was impossible to help him so long as he stayed at home. Not that Dan was to blame, for he would have worked if he could; but no one would employ him. He stands as the representative of many thousands, just like himself, full of good-nature and recklessness, with no habits of obedience, discipline, or order. He had never learned anything since he left school. It was some time before I could venture to emigrate him, and I thank God for that, for it gave us the opportunity of getting him confirmed; and, in the meantime, he brought - one by one - lots of his mates to know us, the most influential of whom, a lad we called "Nobby," suggested that our own house was the only fitting club-room for his mates. And that really was the solution of the difficulty. Every Sunday night he brought, and kept in perfect order, whomsoever he would, and I trace to Dan and Nobby the breaking up of a gang, unkindly called "The Forty Thieves," though very few of them had ever really stolen, yet a real terror to the neighbourhood. Dan is at this present moment a most prosperous person in Canada, with a wife and family. Nobby is a stoker. I hear from both of them from time to time.

The real difficulty of work like this is that it makes tremendous demands on one's own personality, and that the larger part of the expenditure is in vain. And yet one has no right whatsoever to be astonished at this, when we try for a moment to measure all the chances that we have had in life, and then realise that these have never had any chance at all. God has two infallible methods of education - He hopes for everyone, He loves everyone; and yet many live in this world for whom no one hopes and whom no one loves. As the Mission work became heavier, I had to surrender much of this individual work, and then God sent us one who could do it infinitely better than we had ever done it; and, strangely, it was against all my own theories, for this time it was a woman who was to do it. Night after night I have seen her sitting in the midst of those whom decent society utterly refuse to help. On our missing a face, she would answer, quite simply, "Oh, he has gone to gaol for a little! Poor fellow, he cannot help fighting." Or, "The temptation was too great for him, and he took something which did not belong to him." She was the first to welcome him after his trouble, to show him that she had forgotten it; never preaching, never teaching, but with infinite tact dealing, in the truest sense, with their souls. I have prepared many of them for confirmation; I have heard the plain story of their whole lives simply and repentantly told; I have known them get up at six o'clock in the morning, to go and call each other for Communion; I have known them stand any amount of ridicule and temptation; I have seen one stand up for his mate when the rest thought he had brought disgrace on her whom they call "mother," because he knew that that would be "mother's" wish, I see them come home as soldiers

VISIT TO WINCHESTER, 1893

VISIT TO WINCHESTER 1894

and sailors, and from situations that we have got for them at a
distance, in the truest sense refined. I have given them their
Communions after days of earnest struggle against sin, or on the
mornings of their departures; I read as much of their letters as any
eye but hers may read. The world might call it almost miraculous, but
it is a miracle that could be reproduced in any single place, even the
worst, if we workers had but those methods of hope and love.

And God gave me later on another worker, with the same
methods, perhaps in an even more difficult sphere. All boys from
fourteen to sixteen are cruel and disagreeable. Passion, soon to find
itself expressed in their manhood, troubles them, irritates them,
brings forth mischief. Where there is the restraint of home or school,
this is often mitigated, and outwardly the boy looks delightful. Where
there is no restraint, "devilish" is the only adjective that represents
him. Though the most important class for a clergyman to touch,
fearing, as they do, neither God nor man, they remain as a rule
untouched. You may cure them individually, when they reach the age
of twenty, but I always knew that the only sound method of working
would be to *"prevent"* them. All of us at different times tried our
hand on them. All of us failed. I cannot speak of our last trial as
successful, because it only lasted two years, but I believe in my heart
that it would have been successful. It called itself a Brigade, but it
was no more like a Brigade than the Tower Hamlets Militia is like the
Guards. There was a semblance at first in the way of caps, and belts,
and pouches, which I paid for, but Dowglass found that all of that
was more or less, as he would call it, "tommy rot." I remember
bringing some ladies with great pomp to see the drill, when the
leader on the left flank suddenly beat a hurried retreat, but not before
we had seen that, in the exertion of stooping, the braces which kept
together an otherwise disunited pair of trousers had given way. They
were certainly the most ragged, noisy, and disobedient crew that ever
a clergyman gathered together. The vision of one evening last August
is vividly borne in upon my memory. Dowglass had had to go up to
town for the day, and Charlie Davidson, our one-legged gymnast,
who used to give them instruction, was also away. But the Brigade
were not to be thus put off. Some of them effected an entrance into
the gymnasium, and opened the doors for the rest, who swarmed in

and proceeded to turn it upside down. Conibeere tried in vain to stem the torrent, and when I came in from church utterly tired, Looey, who was rushing out to summon aid, nearly fell into my arms, exclaiming, "Thank God, master, you are come. The house is being wrecked." My sudden appearance in their midst produced no effect, except that the missiles, including a leg of the piano, were now directed at me. I hurled them all out into Clarence Street, and shut the doors, but three times did they burst them open.

And yet I am quite sure that, given two or three years' more work, there would have been tremendous results. If the loafer class is ever to be exterminated, if that menace to society, the unemployed, is ever to disappear from the face of the earth, it will only be done by men with large enough hearts and sufficient faith *preventing* the loafer.

In 1886 Mrs. Richardson - I had rather say Mrs. Dick, and I am sure she won't mind - invited me to bring a party of mission men to Winchester to spend the day in College. About sixty went, I having to pay all their railway fares, in some cases even paying them their day's work - false pride on my part, because I did not like College to think we had no men to go. They broke into the warden's garden, and stole his fruit; they climbed over the wall of the bathing-place, and laughed at the men who were learning to swim; they tried to kiss the ladies who waited on them; they most of them got drunk before we went home. Mrs. Dick's invitation is as elastic as her own heart. Year by year more and more men have wanted to go. This year we limited it to a hundred and sixty; we had to refuse an equal number. All of them paid their own journeys, except a few old men out of work, and some of the better-off men clubbed together, so that no expense should fall on the Mission. I don't suppose men ever had a more delightful day. I am quite sure no lady ever entertained a more delightful company. We visited the cathedral, St. Cross, and all the places of interest. We had two splendid meals. One whole day's perfect enjoyment, everyone sober, not a rude or rough word, and yet some of us were the identical people who had gone ten years before, and all of the same class, all the Mission's children.

IV.
Our Womankind.

I UTTERLY disapprove of any club that takes girls systematically away from their own homes. It makes them for the present unmaidenly, and in the future bad wives and mothers," so a very excellent clergyman's wife said to me at the end of one of my lectures. I tried to suggest to her that this was not quite the standard to which she had brought up her own daughters; but she soon answered that by saying, "Oh, that's quite different! my girls are ladies." Thank God I was able to answer her, "My girls are ladies too." For in the truest and most real sense that is what my sisters, and those who have worked with them, have achieved at Landport - ladies in appearance and manners, in mind and in heart. It has been, of course, a slow and tedious process, some disappointments, but surprisingly few as compared with the work among boys and men. "How have you done it?" people have often said to me, when sitting at one of our dances. My sister answers, "By having ideals for them; they soon live up to them."

The good seed had been sown before we came, more efficiently amongst them, I think, than in any other parochial work. Dr. Linklater had started a club for girls called "The Social." Almost all the original members, certainly all who are living in Portsmouth, belong to it still. They alarmed me very much the first time I saw them. I had half expected to be asked to give a short address, but I found them in the middle of a game of dumb-crambo. They very kindly soon put me at my ease by telling me that they did not think my sermons were as good as Dr. Linklater's, but they did it in such a genuine kind way that I could not be offended. Most of them, I found out, worked at the Stay Factory; some of them were in service, and they all either lived in the parish, or had been prepared for confirmation by one of the clergy. My first great quarrel with them was because I thought them too exclusive; and herein is the chief difference between work amongst girls and amongst boys. At first you must be exclusive; you have almost reached a point of perfection when you can afford not to be so. Quite rightly their parents would have objected, and they themselves would have lost caste in the factory, besides running a real danger themselves. Ah! how often one wishes there was the same public opinion amongst men that there is amongst women, and that the shady man had as much difficulty in getting into good society as the shady woman. And yet I felt how utterly useless our woman's work would be if it remained at the point of respectability. The very stay factories from which these girls came were, in those days, places of great temptation. Many of the workers were positively bad, and even amongst those who were not leading bad lives there was great vulgarity of speech and manner, a want of all true refinement. All that is changed today, and our Portsmouth factory girls are, as a rule, most respectable and well-conducted.

Then the Commercial Road and the Southsea Common were a perpetual menace. Those places, in which the girls delighted to walk, were full not only of rollicking, good-natured, thoughtless soldiers and sailors, but of those most hateful of all living creatures, the older profligate, the zest of whose pleasure is the innocence of his victim. Many of these girls, too, see sin continually in the streets in which they live. They see other girls who have no work to do - would to God they knew more plainly the awfulness of the work they do do! - able to dress well and go to places of amusement continually, while they themselves too-often are unable to earn enough to keep themselves in the actual necessaries of life, with a hundred wretched old women ever on the look-out to tell them how easily money can be made. Take a walk any night you like down the Commercial Road, and, however prejudiced you might be against clubs that keep girls away from their own homes, you would be converted. And so our "Social" gradually added to its numbers, became courageous enough to take in one and then another who really wanted a helping hand, and thus led the way for opening two other clubs for younger girls, so that now, I suppose, there are more than a hundred girls attending every week. I can never tell what I owe to my elder girls, many of them

Sunday School teachers and temperance workers, all of them communicants, every one helping a circle of younger girls, the truest, purest, most loving friends I have in the world.

Each club has its nominal lady manager. Miss Brown has governed the " Social" now for twelve years. It would be impossible to even measure the love which binds these girls together, love which proves itself in the highest acts of self-denial. I have known, when there was little doing at the factory, a girl lending another her good bonnet and jacket to come to church in on Sunday, she coming in her workday one. I have known, when another girl was sick, three of them arranging to surrender their own night's rest, that the sick girl might have someone with her at night, though the illness lasted over six weeks. I have known a girl going with Miss Dolling into the worst streets, into the worst houses, looking for one whom we heard had gone astray. This spirit has spread even amongst the younger girls, and with it a spirit of self-respect, which has given them an absence of self-consciousness, and has very largely removed that horrid giggling habit so common amongst them. My sisters and I have taken them to spend the day with friends of our own in the country, as well as with Mrs. Bramston at Winchester - I like to call her Mrs. Trant - who does for the girls and women what Mrs. Richardson does for the boys and men. Wherever we go, their hosts always remark the same things - their naturalness and refinement.

And yet even with all this one felt that there was something wanting. There is a perfect naturalness and fitness in humanity, the want of recognition of which is oftentimes the overthrow of religious work. It is natural and proper for boys and girls to court, for men and women to marry. We had failed altogether with regard to this. We had excellent clubs for boys, excellent clubs for girls, and then just when you thought you had got hold of them your influence weakened. Soon they disappeared, and the reason was perfectly natural; they had begun to "walk out." Then one discovered that the one great difficulty in all this was, that it was literally walking out, they had no place where courtship could be carried out. Two dangers in this will suggest themselves to any thinking person. First, the whole thing, as a rule, was done in secret; secondly, there was no outward moral restraint. To people without deep moral sense of right these two dangers would be very great, and they are the cause of most grievous consequences to large numbers of young people. You would naturally say, "Why cannot they use their own homes?" But if you lived with your father and mother, and many brothers and sisters, in one common feeding room, perhaps you would not be bold enough to present your fiancée. I have often known a marriage take place, and the parents on both sides have never been introduced to their new relative. I have more often known marriages take place because of necessity, when the religious ceremony was looked upon as a kind of whitewash. Naturally one talked a great deal both to boys and girls on the subject of courtship, and they soon showed what was one's duty. We were bound to supply that which the circumstances of their life prevented, an opportunity of meeting and knowing each other. Then came the real difficulty. Where were they to meet, and what were they to do? The gymnasium was the natural meeting place, and so we tried a kind of social evening. But they proved anything but social - the young men on one side of the room, the young ladies on the other. If any male was bold enough to cross over, he was received with giggling, and as conversation was not our strong point - for we had never been taught, so to speak, to talk - he soon subsided, red-faced, amongst his fellows. Then we tried games, but they always ended in horrid romps. All games seemed to end in kissing, and forfeits brought forth witticisms which were not always conducive to propriety. At last my sister was bold enough to suggest, what had been on the tip of my tongue for weeks, why should they not dance? The girls had already learned in their own clubs. But excellent and good-natured as our girls are, we feared it would be putting their kindness to a hard test to ask them to become instructors, especially as all our men could not bring dancing pumps; and though a hob-nailed boot is very useful for most men's daily work, it was not a pleasant reminder to a partner that she was good-natured enough to be dancing for the purpose of teaching someone else to dance. So I cleared out my dining-room one or two nights a week, and we taught the men as my sisters had taught the girls, and now for the last five years our dancing-class has been one of the most valuable parish institutions. Mr. Whittick, our blind organist, presides at the piano. Nearly all the members are communicants. I had to make this rule, because I must be able to stand over the character of every member. Everyone pays twopence, and we dance from 8 till 10.30 p.m.

It is extraordinary, the difference which this has effected in the manners of our people. The dancing is, perhaps, a little more serious than at a ball in Belgravia, for squares are danced with a due attention to the figures. It has given one the most happy opportunity of enabling our boys and girls to meet naturally together, and I am more and more convinced by experience that one of the greatest causes of sin, in places like ours, is this want. Many of our boys and girls have got engaged to be married through this chance, and if any of them get engaged to a girl outside the parish, the dance gives then an excellent excuse to introduce her to us. It would be very difficult to say, "You must come and see my parson." It is very easy to say, "You must come and see my dancing-class." In the last six years I do not think we have had one marriage amongst our people for which we have had cause to feel shame. In the last four years I do not think any of our people have been married without receiving the Holy Communion on the Sunday before, or on the morning of their marriage. Why cannot we talk far more plainly on these subjects to our people? This hideous demand for facilities for divorce, the extraordinary attitude of almost the whole episcopate to it, could never have arisen if we had taught plainly that marriage is a Sacrament, in which God gives grace enabling people to live in holy love together, and therefore demanding from people a preparation as rigid, I need not say more rigid, perhaps, than the preparations needed for the reception of other Sacraments. Think of the hideous vulgarity of modern marriages, the whole talk about clothes and feasting. Think of the behaviour in church. Amongst fashionable people the ceremony is as interesting as a Drawing-room. Amongst my class of people the ceremony is disfigured by ribald jests, oftentimes by the rudest horse-play. Our Lord not only consecrated by His own presence, but brought His Blessed Mother to Cana of Galilee as well. Oh, inestimable value of any saintly woman, who can show the girl why there need not be any amazement in the commencement of a new life, in which, unless she is prepared, there must be a strange and awful awakening.

Then the influence we gained amongst the girls reacted very much on their own homes. I had been very anxious about the elder women, for though, when I came, I found three mothers' meetings, they were badly attended, and I was told that different streets would not amalgamate, for, in our little parish, there is just as much difference between one street and another as there is between Earl's Court and West Kensington. I felt that this unchristian state of things must, at all hazards, be broken down, and that the best method was to try and make the meeting as much like a party as possible. And so the first use we made of the schoolroom attached to the gymnasium was to open it once a week, and, as numbers increased, twice a week, for a kind of At Home. At first it was difficult to make them understand that they need not bring a piece of work if they did not like. They might talk to each other, indeed gossip, and move about the room when there was no singing or reading going on, and there always was a cup of tea and a piece of bread and butter. I heard a lady once, when I was lecturing, saying aside to a friend, as I spoke about this, "Fancy, encouraging them in their gossiping habits. Of course they will come if he gives them tea." When the lecture was over I happened to stand behind her for a minute or two in the crush, and I can vouch for two cups of tea, several cakes, and a story to her neighbour, which I should call gossip. Do you suppose that there would be any afternoon visiting if there was no gossip and no afternoon tea? I should admire the courage of the lady who cared to make the attempt.

Of course our influence over these women was slow. On our first summer outing, seventy of us went to the Isle of Wight. It happened to be a very wet day, perhaps that was the excuse, but I noticed in many of their pockets, when coming home, the outline of a little bottle, the contents of which one could easily guess at by the ardour with which these old ladies skipped, for one had supplied a skipping rope, and by the character of the songs they sang. Luckily for us this was an impediment to quick disembarking, and so my sisters and I were glad to get off the boat, before we could be recognised as the guardians of the party. But soon all that passed away. Letting them talk gave us an opportunity of showing them what conversation might be made, above all showing them that vulgarity is seldom witty and never convenient. In 1894 they willingly gave up their summer outing, their one yearly enjoyment, to add to a fund which we were raising for the sufferers from the *Victoria* disaster. Women are far more stay-at-home, and get far fewer treats than men, and therefore it was a great self-denial.

The girls, as I have said, soon induced their mothers to come, and thus we got an influence in the family. The vast majority of our mothers are regular communicants now, influencing their husbands and sons, giving me immediate warning when any spot in the parish is getting bad, with their Coal Club, their Blanket Club, their Penny Bank, carrying into every street in the parish the power of a homely religious influence, and paying back to me and mine tenderness, sympathy, and love, which people could only do who have become in the truest sense religious and refined. Remember how almost impossible it is to conquer old habits long indulged, how cursing, and swearing, and drinking, and bad talk take even deeper root in women's hearts than in men's, and just because their lives are far more commonplace, these are the harder to eradicate. I wish I dare tell you of how bravely month after month some have fought against some special besetting sin, coming to me regularly before Communion Sunday to report progress, so humbly, so trustfully. As I write these words, a letter comes from Portsmouth, "I hope you will be able to save many poor souls, as you have saved me. My husband says he hopes I will not break the pledge now you are gone, as he has had four years of comfort. But I will pray for the help of God to keep me up. I was at church this morning at eight, a very few. We are going to have service on Wednesday at a quarter to six, so that will give us all a chance to go. I remain your affectionate child in Christ." (She is more than sixty.) This is only one out of a hundred miracles that the Blessed Sacrament has wrought among us. For years that woman had fought against Confirmation. It was the Blessed Sacrament that broke down the stubbornness of her heart.

I can hardly bear to think of them now, for I know how especially desolate they are. And yet I know that their lessons have not been learned in vain, and that as long as they have the Blessed Sacrament, the supernatural graces which have refined them will still support and strengthen them. Many of them are very old, all of them are very ignorant, very poor. I wish you could see them at their day's outing at

Winchester, enjoying the rest and the beauty, so grateful for every attention, so careful not to appear greedy, and yet to do, as one said, "graceful justice" to the splendid food provided; or, better still, if you could see them at their own special service in church, in the truest sense at home in their Father's house, their house, too, because it is His, and because some act of self-denial on their part has helped to build it; their dear old cracked voices singing all out of tune, their little sighing "Amens" and "Halleluias" in the middle of the prayer, their rapt attention during the sermon, the tear or the smile as the case might be, with sometimes a comment thrown in; a little impatience on the part of the younger, when the clock is reaching four, because the children will be home; a long lingering, sometimes for hours, on the part of those who live alone.

V.
Our Children.

THE real answer to the loafer and the prostitute is the
environment of the children. It is almost impossible to cure; it is,
comparatively speaking, easy to prevent. And so, if we are going to
make any real effort towards removing these two national disgraces
and dangers, it must be in the treatment of our children. Even then
you have fatal odds against you, for heredity marks down many for
its own prey, and it will take many generations before heredity will be
conquered. But environment may be improved, and I contend that
every man and woman, who tries to train their children properly,
creates the needed environment. If only we could reform the parents
there would be very little difficulty about the children, and I believe
that the truest measure of all work like ours is the care that parents
take about their children. While the mother is actually nursing her
child she will make for it every possible sacrifice, but, alas! as the
well-springs of nourishment dry up, the well-springs of love dry up
too, and you will oftentimes wonder why Almighty God gave such
mothers so many children. Poverty and uncertainty as to wages have
a good deal to do with the parents' difficulty in disciplining their
children. I wonder if well-to-do people ever consider these mothers.
They have no servants; however ill they feel there is no one to do
anything for the children but themselves; headaches, lassitude, even
the knowledge of impending sickness, is for them no excuse. They
have no strengthening diet, no power to satisfy the common wants of
their children in food or clothes; no baize doors between the nursery
and the bedroom. I speak advisedly of the mother alone as the trainer
of her children, because the father, in work, has no time, out of work
no heart. My wonder is, not that they slave so little for their children,
but rather that they slave so much. Religion alone can mend all this -

I have seen it work miracles in homes - the belief that the child is God's gift, that He is its Father, that He will give her strength for her every need, and that the prayer, "Give us this day our daily bread," God will answer. My truest joy at Landport were these converted homes, but even these homes, and far more the homes of the careless, necessitate something more for the children. Religion quickens within the mother the power of creating a true environment round the child; but, alas! after ten years there are many parents untouched by religion in our parish. Of course we have done what we could with our Sunday School, though there is no greater mistake than to suppose that the Sunday School can in any way take the place of the home school. Our Sunday School has never attracted very many children. My desire has been to train a few children well, and the preserving of discipline, and insistence on outward reverence, in a parish like ours made our Sunday School unpopular; a mother once said to one of my sisters,

"I shan't let my boys go to your school any longer, because kneeling wears out the knees of their trousers."

A child, who had lately joined, said to another sister, " I am leaving your school for the one round the corner, because you go to your treat in the train, and the other school goes in brakes."

I do not suppose that we have ever had more than five or six hundred children in it, but thanks to a most excellent staff of teachers, many of whom have been with us all the ten years, our children are in perfect order, and answer extraordinarily well. "We have always thought, too, that it was far more important for a child to come to the Children's Celebration at ten o'clock than to the afternoon instruction. Indeed we very soon discovered that this ten o'clock celebration was the most important religious factor in the whole parish. It has been maintained oftentimes with great personal difficulty; I have often myself had to say four Masses on Sunday, and, until the Rev. John Elwes came to help us, one of us had always had to say two; but we felt that no amount of inconvenience could be a possible excuse for depriving our children of this most necessary factor in their religious education. Assuredly we have been well repaid.

I bless God for many things at S. Agatha's, but for none more than the dignity of the younger acolytes, dear Barratt's earnest leading of the children, the singing of the older girls who composed the choir, and the reverent behaviour of all the children, even the infants taking part in every word that was said or sung, thus enabling us to make the children's service their chief education in all religion. If this service should ever be given up, I should indeed fear for the future of S. Agatha's. With us the Sunday School has the merit of being perfectly voluntary, parents, as a rule, taking no trouble about making their children come; as long as they get rid of them they do not care whether they go to Sunday School or not, and, unless you have to punish a child, the parent often remains to you an unknown quantity.

All this made us very anxious to acquire Day Schools, and, like everything else, God sent them to us, when we were ready for them. One little corner of our district had been cut off, because the mother parish wished to preserve her schools, built in the year 1823. In 1889 they had fallen into such decay that they were practically unfit for use, and were condemned by the Education Department. The then vicar offered them to the Board. I saw at once that God meant me to take them. I called all our people together, and told them that the real difficulty was money, for I should have to lay out £1000 on the schools immediately. I knew, of course, that they could subscribe no money, but we have ever found at S. Agatha's that praying people are more potential than giving people. They decided that they would devote one day a month to perpetual prayer, beginning at half-past five in the morning and continuing till ten at night. We have kept that custom up ever since. It is an extraordinary sight to see poor ignorant people coming in for their half-hour's prayer, each one responsible for their own time, and, if they cannot attend, sending someone else, so that the chain of intercession is never broken. Sometimes in the afternoon, when the women have leisure, or in the evening, when work is all over, there are fifty to a hundred people all praying silently for what we need. The Blessed Sacrament is reserved all day, and the poorest bring their flowers to deck the altar. No spot in the world will ever be so beautiful to me as that little flower-covered altar. At any rate the intercession worked the first miracle for us, for in just over two months we had collected the £1000 we needed for the first outlay upon the schools, and the getting of this money was all the more wonderful because there was such a strong feeling in the diocese, and elsewhere, against us. I insert a letter received from the Bishop of Guildford, himself a most ardent supporter of Church Schools, which you will see was not intended for publication, but which his Lordship has very kindly allowed me to publish, as a proof of how really miraculous it was that we got that sum.

"The Close," Winchester,
"October 30, 1889.
"Dear Mr. Dolling, - I have not answered your letter hurriedly because I wanted to think over it before I did so. The pleasantest plan for me personally would be simply to accede to your request, but I cannot reconcile it to my conscience to do so. It may perhaps already have struck you that I have not responded to appeals for pecuniary help for your mission. This has not arisen from inadvertence. I am always ready and glad to do all I can as regards Episcopal or Archidiaconal ministrations in your parish, and I can honestly say that the confirmation which I held in your chapel was one of intense interest to me. I can also perfectly honestly wish you heartily 'God speed' in your work, and honour you for your work's sake. But I do long that the views which you hold were not of the very extreme character which, judging from utterances which I occasionally see in print, they are; and that the ritual which you think it your duty to carry out were of a simpler character than it is, and used in accordance with the wishes of our own Bishop, who certainly does not make a man an offender for a word. I need not enlarge upon this point, but, feeling it as I do very strongly, I could not conscientiously *help forward* a scheme which would bring the children of the district referred to under your direct church teaching. It seems to me a wholly different thing for me in my position as Suffragan to come and minister in Holy things as a Bishop to those who are, as a fact, under your spiritual charge, and by my own free act and deed to endeavour to bring your influence to bear upon children who are not as yet, at any rate ecclesiastically, a portion of your flock. I hope you will give me credit for thus acting from conscientious motives, and

believe that I can still quite truly and unfeignedly pray that a blessing may rest upon your labours, and that all our mistakes and errors may be pardoned and over-ruled for good.

"I am, dear Mr. Dolling,
"Always yours very truly,
"GEORGE HENRY GUILDFORD,
"REV. R. DOLLING."

In all, the schools have cost me over £3000; but they have a splendid record, and I do not grudge one single penny. In 1889 the average attendance was 350, the Government grant £276; in 1895 the average attendance was 519, the grant £476. Let me say, at once, this was due to our teachers. Never have any schools had such devoted teachers, their one object in view not the gaining of the grant, but the moral character of the child.

The ease with which my sisters and others have been able to mould our younger girls into their present excellent state, is very largely due to the splendid foundation laid by Mrs. Berrow, the mistress of the girls. Her indefatigable labours during many years in which she has managed the girls' school, are beyond all praise. Over and over again, when in utter amazement I have said to a girl, "Who warned you of that danger which you have been able to avoid? Who put before you that path of duty which you have had the grace to follow?" the answer was, "Oh, Mrs. Berrow, of course!" The "of course" is so characteristic, because it just shows how perfectly naturally the most difficult duty was performed. I would that I had words to express the gratitude I feel to this most Christian lady.

When our boys' school had reached its lowest ebb, discipline and teaching having been twice condemned by the Inspector, I asked my dear friend Saunders, whose father was a very valued friend of mine, to lead a forlorn hope in the boys' school. The ardour with which he commenced his work has never for a single moment slackened. He found the school the worst in the town. I leave it under his management, one of the very best. But I do not value his teaching powers so much as his influence over the boys' futures. He has created a school library and a school band. He has managed for three years the best continuation school in the whole district. The Bible-

OUR BAND

class, into which he gathers on Sunday the lads who have left him, is one of the most valuable helps to religion in the whole parish. It would vex them if I were to tell you of the extraordinary sacrifices they have made for S. Agatha's schools; but, as I believe God gave me the schools, so I believe He gave me my head teachers, and the rest of the school staff; and I am confident, as long as the schools remain under their management, there will ever be an influence amongst those of the flock most dear to our Lord, such as He Himself desires His little ones should be affected by.

No one can measure what England owes to the Board Schools; it would have been impossible for the Church to have kept pace with the increase of population, and with the new thought, which has not yet been half realised, that every child has a right to the best education. But there is one truth that I am sure we shall all, sooner or later, hold - it is not the business of the State to teach religion. If some means could be devised by which each denomination might appoint teachers to give the religious instruction, the education difficulty might be solved. But we are told this is impossible - an impossibility, I fear, arising largely from the laziness and jealousy of those who ought to be the religious teachers. If religion is taught in a school it is the most vital of all subjects; it needs the most skilful handling, the most God-sought and God-given tact, and yet it is just the one subject upon which no enquiry can be made as to the fitness of its teachers. In fact, it is possible for a child to be taught by teachers of every, and of no, religious opinions. Then there is no such thing as unsectarian religion: the very words are contradictory. Every teacher has his own bias, and he would be more than human if he did not convey this to the children. People think that this does not matter, because children are too young to understand, or because such teaching can do them no harm. But it is far easier to teach a dogmatic truth than to make a child understand, or gain any benefit from, a whole chapter of the Bible. To hold up Christ as an example, and His words as precepts, and not to teach the child the method by which Christ conveys to him the power of copying the example, is a cruel wrong. I believe even in many Church Schools there has been a great want of definite teaching. We have taught far too much, yet far too little - far too much about the Old Testament and the services of the Church; far too little about those saving truths which even quite young children can apprehend, and assimilate to themselves. Just before Christmas we were asked to take in a little soldier from Aldershot, a lad of about sixteen. His father and mother had died when he was four. An uncle, who played a whistle outside public-houses in the southern parts of Scotland, had adopted him. When he came to us he said that, until he had joined the army, six months before, he had never slept three consecutive nights in the same place; indeed, most nights a doorstep or a hayrick had been his bed. It is almost impossible to conceive a worse bringing up. On Sunday he went to church with our own boys; and Conibeere, who looks after them, remarked, on coming out of church, "I think he must be a Roman Catholic, because he was so reverent." Alas! soldiers, sailors, and tramps coming from all parts of England are seldom reverent. That Sunday night he told me all about himself. It was almost impossible to believe that so pure a soul should have matured under circumstances so adverse, but he had a talisman that had never failed him; he had never forgotten the few soul-saving truths he had learned as a little child. Bishop Virtue, the Roman Catholic Bishop of Portsmouth, very kindly confirmed him, and now the little man is on his way to India. But he wrote us before he sailed that he would never forget S. Agatha's, for there he had first learned what a home was. He knew nothing about the Bible, Old or New Testament; but he knew what repentance meant, what prayer meant, what communion meant. He knew it so thoroughly that neither the temptations of the street nor of the barrack-room had robbed him of it. Surely that is what we ought to teach every child. Let us recognise that some children are born religious - I mean they love the Bible and the lives of the saints; they have a power of expressing much fervour - I do not know that they are always the best children - and they will certainly acquire all the unnecessary part of religion. But every child has the capacity for acquiring the necessary part, and surely it is the duty of the Church to see that all her children have the chance of its acquirement. Every energy is now being put forth by the Church to retain, or even to increase, her schools. Thirty years ago she had almost the whole of the schools of England in her hands. Was she true to her enormous chance? Did she turn out Churchmen and

Churchwomen? Are the Sacraments frequented to-day by those whom she taught? In all honesty let us face this question, "Why this anxiety to-day? and let us earnestly pray Almighty God that it means her united effort to teach her children as they ought to be taught, refusing to accept diocesan schemes that insist on an amount of teaching altogether unnecessary and superfluous; and, above all, the getting rid of that hideous system of examinations which ruins not only religious, but all secular, education.

Measure the increase in good education which has taken place since the passing of the Education Act, and every true Englishman will surely rejoice. Recognise that all that the State ought to do is to teach secular education. If the Church, by possessing schools, can help the State in this matter, and therefore get a better opportunity of teaching her own children, let her rejoice, but let her recognise her twofold responsibility, that the religious education must be ample and complete, the secular education the best that can be given. If she fails in either of these two duties she has no right to remain a teacher, and it would be fatal to her duty if, for the sake of gaining a little money, and thereby lessening the continual burden of subscription, she either gives an inferior education, or has inferior buildings, unsanitary or such like, which the State should not for a moment permit, or else allows some outside control to interfere with the religion which she is bound to teach, or with her method of appointing teachers. It is easy to accept unfettered money from a Conservative Government, but no party remains in power very long in England, and the taking of money now may possibly be an excuse for another Government to enforce its own terms. I had the honour to serve on the School Board in Portsmouth for three years. I know the zeal and energy with which its members manage the schools in the town. I am grateful beyond expression for the benefits they have conferred on education in Portsmouth. I confess that their energy has been the incentive to all the Church Schools to progress, for they set a standard of education which is extremely useful to the whole district. But I, for one, would far rather have seen them merely imparting secular knowledge. I believe that, if we knew that no religious teaching was given, every Dissenting minister and every Church clergyman would throw far greater energy into the work of teaching religion to their own children. I believe that oftentimes the knowledge that religion is taught is a salve to the conscience, an excuse not to realise our duty towards our children far more than we do. It is an awful thought, that of a Godless England. It is a thought that should strike terror into the conscience of every single man, whether he be cleric or laic; yet I believe that there are thousands of children to-day who, if a year after they leave school were questioned about their religion, would, as far as actual knowledge went, be discovered to be Godless.

My service on the Board, I think, taught me another benefit in Church Schools. The daily visit of the clergy and other Church workers is not only an enormous encouragement to the teachers, but creates altogether a more humane atmosphere. It tends, too, to more softened ways and more refined manners on the part of the children, and it gives often a greater opportunity for getting work for children and keeping a hold over them when they have left school. I think that there were a few members of the Board who tried to do something in this way, but the most of us were far too busy. I am told that under the London School Board this omission is corrected by a system of managers, who are in touch both with the children and the teachers. I fear in the Portsmouth Board we should have been jealous of delegating any authority. I believe, too, that if there had been a more personal touch between the members of the Board and the teachers, several little difficulties, which have lately arisen, would have disappeared. Indeed, I blame myself very much that during my three years' service I did not get more personally acquainted with the teachers, though I threw open my gymnasium twice a week to the younger ones, and many joined our debating society. The increase of population in Portsmouth has been so abnormal, that the expenditure of the Board in creating places and plant has necessarily been very great, and consideration for the ratepayers' pockets is the reason why our salaries do not compare favourably with those in like-sized towns. And there were some other little vexatious arrangements, which I believe more personal intercourse between the Board and the teachers could easily have re-arranged.

I say all this because I am conscious that the two difficulties which Englishmen must face with regard to the Board School question are these - first, that the State cannot, and therefore ought not to be expected to, teach religion; and secondly, that a danger exists in all elected bodies that they may become merely machines, and so create in those they employ a merely mechanical habit of performing their duties.

VI.
Our Penitentiary Work.

WHEN society is brave enough to say a "fallen man," as well as a "fallen woman," the so-called fallen woman will soon disappear. Alas! we talk so glibly of young men's "wild oats," oftentimes speaking of sin as a necessity, as if to do wrong in this direction, being human, is natural, that it has become almost recognised that the so-called fallen woman is a necessity. This kind of thing was said over and over again to me by clergymen and others, when I talked to them about the state in which I found my parish, until I was forced to recognise that I must look at this question from two points of view - first, the reclaiming of the sinner; secondly, the removing from amongst my own children the awful danger of infection. I want you to pray, before you read this chapter, that no word of mine may hurt or wound you, as I am praying God the Holy Ghost to give me grace to write it bravely and wisely.

As far as the reformation of this sinner goes, it can only be effected by the loving compassion of a good woman, and God sent me in the hour of my need a woman who practically worked miracles. She is dead now, so I may call her by her name, Mrs. Waldron, a sister of Prebendary Grier. She lived in one of the little cottages which now form the site of the new church, weak in body, yet of such an untiring courage and energy that I have often known her for more than twelve hours at a stretch without food or rest, labouring for some poor soul. I gave her carte blanche when she came, asking no questions, discussing no case unless she desired to discuss it with me, but I know that in a short time more than a hundred poor girls had made their determination for a better life under her influence. And it was no wonder, for harder than marble would have been the heart that resisted her love. In the lives of the saints one reads of those who, nursing the lepers, rejoiced to kiss their sores. That is a physical action, which I suppose anybody could accustom themselves to do. But to touch with your soul a leprous soul, to bear with the blasphemy, the vulgarity, of those who have lost all shame, and perhaps never have had any, to bear with it continually day by day, to have your kindness and hospitality repaid by having all your things stolen, and yourself flouted to your face, mocked at and derided; to find that poor one sick and tired just at the moment when change is possible, to bring her home again without one word or even look of reproach, to do it all without any excitement, any telling of it to anyone else, loving the most hideous for the dear Lord's sake, treating them in the dear Lord's own way, no wonder the success was phenomenal. And joined to this an even harder work, to persuade parents to allow their children, their girls of ten and eleven and twelve, to go into preventive homes. For when we first went to Landport that was the only solution of the difficulty possible. We discovered many, many little children from whom no secret of sin was hidden and we could not remove in a moment their awful instructors, who, directly they were old enough, and that age came sometimes as young as thirteen or fourteen, would give them an easy opportunity of turning instruction into practice. So, though I have never myself been in favour of taking children from their own homes, there was nothing else that we could do.

I determined that by God's help I would not only endeavour to get the girls out of the bad houses, but the houses out of the parish. The present law is so very difficult to put in force, that I felt that, even if I was successful in invoking the law in a few instances, I should create great prejudice against the work, and effect practically very little reform. So by degrees, with the help of my sister and some of our most earnest mothers, I got a complete list of all the bad houses in the parish. I wrote to all the owners, taking for granted that they did not know the bad purposes for which their houses were being used. I have written these letters week after week, in the hope of shaming them by my persistency or worrying them into taking some steps. After a time, I generally wrote to the Superintendent of Police, and he very kindly did all he could. If there were little children in the house,

Mr. Silk, the School Board officer, was also an efficient helper. Then at last the owner, wearied or ashamed, as a rule gave notice to his tenant, and thus in detail, and one by one, our plague spots were removed, until just before I left the parish I bought for £250 the only bad house remaining. The poor woman, now in a lunatic asylum, was her own landlady, and that was why it was so difficult to move it.

You will be quite sure that every effort was made by dealing personally with all the inmates, for when Mrs. Waldron left us, one of my sisters undertook this special work. It would be unbecoming of me to speak of her tact and tenderness; nay, by reason of the salutary rule we had of never talking over cases, I hardly know of them myself; all that I do know is that no poor girl ever left my parish without having the truest womanly love offered her - love which, after seeking her in the worst streets of the town, often found her in the wards of the hospital or poor-house; love which she had refused in the day of her strength, and which now triumphed in the day of her weakness.

Of course, this cleansing of our parish produced a great deal of ill-will from owners of property. Once, feeling myself bound to make a statement in one of my sermons, which got into a newspaper, I was threatened with a libel action for £10,000. I remember quite well, when the lawyer came to see me about it, his utter astonishment not only when he discovered that what I had said was true, but even more when the thought was revealed to him that a clergyman need not necessarily be a fool, and the readiness with which he and his client abated the nuisance was beyond all praise.

The abatement of these nuisances soon did away with the necessity of our sending children to preventive homes. Some words that I had spoken during my first year's work induced a lady, who has since become one of the Mission's dearest friends, to undertake an Orphanage for S. Agatha's children. She opened with a little home in North End, which accommodated about eight children. This was soon overcrowded, and a dear friend of mine, Mrs. Kane, offered us, free of rent, a splendid house in Castle Road, Southsea, where for the last eight years this lady has been mother to more than twenty children. Like all other of God's gifts to us, this house came at the very moment when we wanted it. It is impossible for me to describe the love with which these children have been mothered, and I doubt if anywhere in England there is any like institution, which is so thoroughly a home. Like all other institutions - and yet that word institution itself is its own condemnation, indeed, I do not think it has ever been an institution - it has had its ups and downs, and we have had to accommodate the method of working it to the age of the children. The younger children coming to our own day schools were kept a little in touch with the outside world, though this had its difficulties, for I have known a time when four or five of the choirboys fell violently in love with the girls. But I welcomed even this danger, from the knowledge that the mixing with other children made the girls more humane, and Wally Kimber, aged nine, surreptitiously offering an apple, had his necessary use. There were also the dangers of measles, whooping cough, etc., but I looked upon these as a development of the child's physical character.

While recognising to its very full the need of our Orphanage, for most of our children were orphans, or practically so, because their fathers were sailors, I still hold that an indifferent natural home is better for the child than the best artificial one. There is a give and take, a certain amount of bullying, a having to put up with things as they are, sometimes very needless things, a stinting in diet, above all a development of ministry, that I believe to be almost impossible except in the natural home. All this is a formation of character which enables the girl, as soon as she goes out in the world, to know her own value, to judge for herself, and not to be dependent on rules concerning every point, which private judgment would far more healthily direct. Above all, she learns from her father and brothers, and from their companions and friends, natural intercourse with men, which prevents the first man she sees, after she has gone into service, being an overwhelming attraction.

I hope these words will not sound very ungracious towards the very many kind ladies who have taken our children into their Preventive Homes - I bless God continually for many a girl whom their kindness has saved from utter ruin, both of body and soul - and I think they themselves will agree with me generally in what I say. But, on the other hand, many parents are very glad to be saved the expense and trouble of bringing up children in the days when they

OUR ORPHANS

cannot earn. They even go further than this. I remember, years ago, a great triumph of Mrs. Waldron, when she prevailed on a father to sign the paper allowing his girl to go into a Home. A few months afterwards he came, as I thought, to thank me for having made provision for his child - the mother we knew was a thoroughly bad character - but, after a few preliminaries, he calmly demanded that I should pay him something, or else he would remove the girl, I very soon removed him; but he was continually annoying the sister in charge of the Home, and, as soon as the girl was fifteen, and able to earn, he brought her back again to Portsmouth. I thank God that she was wise enough to insist upon going into service, and has kept herself all right; but it might have been just the other way. Of course, if a mother is depraved, or a girl is beginning to make friends with really bad characters, there is, I suppose, no other remedy; but I am glad to think that, as a rule, such needs have largely passed away from our parish.

We owe a special debt of gratitude to the Portsmouth Ladies' Committee for Fallen and Preventive work. Through their indefatigable secretary, Mrs. Breton, they have taken out of our hands many of our most difficult cases. I know how often a clergyman's work is marred by the kind of pompous officialism of many Penitentiary workers. I wish they could have the happiness of working with either Sister Margaret, of the Deaconesses Home, or with Miss Young, of the little Penitentiary in Somers Road, Southsea. Naturally, we came most in contact with her; for when, on Mrs. Waldron's departure, I shut up our own Penitentiary, hers was open to us night and day. She is, perhaps, the most unassuming and gentle person that ever lived - very delicate, for she was nearly killed in a railway accident, four years ago, and yet exercising a most extraordinary influence over even the rudest and most boisterous girls. The remembrance of her tact and utter absence of hideous rules emboldens me to say what has often been upon my mind about penitentiaries generally - Could there not be a great deal more individualism? And, above all, could there not be fewer prayers and hours of silence? I remember, in my parish in London, a poor girl, who, after many weeks of persuasion, at length entered a temporary Home. On her journey down to a two years' Home in the country, she disappeared. Two days after, a railway porter brought me a shawl that one of the Penitentiary ladies had lent her, with the message, "Tell Mr. Dolling I could not stick all the prayers." Perhaps even you and I, who call ourselves religious, would find three set times for prayers a day, with one or two silent hours, more than we could "stick." And, then, surely a great deal more use might be made of digging. It is far easier to sweat out your evil humours and your sloth in a garden under the sky, than in a wash-house under a roof. I know the infinite tenderness of Penitentiary workers; I know the devotion of their lives; but it has struck me oftentimes, from talking with girls who had been in Homes, that there is a great danger of their looking upon the girl as created for the Home rather than the Home for the girl; and I am sure that if accommodation and workers render this individualism impossible, a smaller number, of whose cure there might be more reasonable assurance, would serve the end far more than a larger number not so successfully dealt with. Above all, a protest needs to be made against a novel system of three months' Homes. There are in all these girls' lives times when either weakness of body, utter poverty, reaction against the hatefulness of their life, or a bitter heart-disappointment - for these poor children still have hearts - prompt them to go to a Home. By all means let there be temporary Homes, where they can be taken in, but for God's sake do not let a whitewashing certificate lightly get them into a house as a servant unless the mistress knows all about them. Of course, there are many ladies living alone who could do no more Christlike act than to give such a girl a chance; but I have known them sometimes in nurseries - I wonder if people realise how soon little children can be injured by bad habits - and I have known them in houses where there are growing-up sons and daughters, worse for the latter than the former.

I hope you will pardon me for these two digressions, but my work in Portsmouth has brought me in contact with so many poor girls whom a Home seems to have hardened, and my work in the confessional has brought me in contact with so many penitents, whose first temptations to sin arose in their earliest days, and were generally suggested by servants.

VII.
Our House.

I HAVE told you that Chance Street was the worst street in the parish, and therefore was the place where I felt I ought to live. But I thank God now that I did not go there at first, for, from the experience of four different houses, I learned the kind of house to build. First of all we lived in Spring Street, but we were soon squeezed out of that. Three of my old London boys appeared almost as soon as we had settled there. Then we had to provide room for Winchester men, and for all sorts of stray guests. One great help we had already gained there, Mary, who has been our housekeeper all through the ten years; but even her fertile imagination could not create bedrooms, and when I had been driven from the bath-room, where I had slept in the bath for two or three nights, to the landing outside, I felt I must see about moving. Naturally you will say, "Why burden yourself with these people? But, I thank God, that during the ten years I have been at the Mission we have never sent away from the door anyone whom we thought we could benefit. To-day I got a letter from India from the first boy we ever sent into the Army - now a collar-maker in the Royal Artillery. He worked in a biscuit factory. His father and mother were dead. He kept himself, board and lodging, on 4s. a week. Sometimes we called him "Dodger," because he stuttered and stammered; sometimes "My Lord," because he was so consequential. I remember once finding him crying in the corner, and I found it was from sheer starvation. There was only one hope for him - three or four months' food and exercise. It cost me, perhaps, £5. Think of it - £5 - and a man made by it. He wrote me to-day, "I have lost my home, when you left Portsmouth, but, thank God, I have not lost you." And then another, one of those strange phenomena out of the slums, in appearance and lack of energy a gentleman, so

LIPTON'S BOYS

attractive, yet so disheartening, needing three years of continued watchfulness and unceasing prayer, to-day a prosperous steward on the Australian line.

And so the family began, not willingly, but of necessity, and when Spring Street was outgrown, then the Mission House in Conway Street was ready for us. There, too, we began another great expense, but blessed beyond all cost - the daily dinner. What hundreds of little children have grown to be men by it! How many working men have been coaxed by it back to health and bread-winning for their family! What a test it has been for tramps and for the unworthy! You can always measure the loafer by the fashion of his eating. What a school for learning truths about humanity - there where tongues were loosened under the influence of hospitality. With knife and fork in hand all men are at ease together, and so we learned to know them, and they to know us. The best school for our fellow priests, for the gentlemen who came down to learn something of this life, and for the Winchester men, has always been our dining-room. Sometimes I know I have marred it myself, for oftentimes when one is ill in body and ill in temper - who shall tell where one begins and the other ends? - my own moroseness has hindered the power of the lesson. But I have known, even in my worst days, a charm that has soothed me back to geniality. If I had been Saul, and David eating before me, it would have been more potential than playing on the harp. Over and over again I have seen the look of polite horror and disdain passing out of some cultured face, when the owner discovered that the shoeblack next him was quite as intelligent as himself. And then the splendid discipline of it all, that power of banter so cleansing for the priggish, that power of laughter so health-giving to the morose, chasing away the frown of set purpose fixed on the face. Eight long years of that common dining-table cost enormous sums of money, and entailed continuous outpouring of strength and of tact; but I doubt if, in all England, money has been better spent, and strength better expended.

Then, too, began the realisation of the danger of a sailor's life. No words of mine are too strong to express the admiration I feel for Miss Weston's magnificent social work. I doubt if there be one woman in England to whom England owes so much. But, surely, we had some

duty towards them too, many of them on board the training-ship
through our instrumentality, many recommended to us by clergymen
who knew them. But all we could do then was one afternoon in the
week, and Sunday afternoon; we had no room for more. With that we
were content until we found that there were some boys who had no
homes to go to for the Christmas holiday, and some who, having
ceased to be boys, and, coming on shore, were led down, because
they had no helping hand, to sin and death. That convinced us that
we must move into a larger house.

My sisters, too, living a little distance from the parish, had found
their work so increased that one felt it was a duty to relinquish the
Mission House to them, and to move into a wretched cottage that we
had bought in Clarence Street, next the Gymnasium, the walls damp,
the floors rotten. Here we lived until the doctor discovered that I was
getting very ill, and Mrs. Porter, who helped Mary, pushed her leg
through the floor of my bedroom into my sitting-room below. Then
we were forced to build. The house next door to that little cottage was
a bad house, a shocking scandal left in the midst of a district
otherwise nearly cleansed. We thought that there would be no
difficulty in buying it, but the owner put a premium on its shameful
success, and I felt that to buy it at the price demanded was only to
abet and encourage sin. Luckily my architect, Mr. Ball, was the most
patient and resourceful of men. Schools, parsonage, and church, all
testify to his extraordinary cleverness, and he devised a plan by
which we utilised the gallery of the Gymnasium for bedrooms, and
were able to make an excellent parsonage. In the place of chief
honour, because she ministered most to the comfort of our house, we
placed the cook and our kitchen, and magnificently she fulfilled her
charge, cooking, with the help of her friend, Looey, for an average of
certainly not less than eighteen every single day, dining and teaing
more than forty upon Sunday, a kind of miracle-worker, never
requiring to know how many were coming, yet always enough for all
who came. And then such splendid sleeping accommodation; four
cubicles, one Winchester room, two other rooms with three beds
each, and soon, because we had overstepped that accommodation, a
long gallery built over one side of the Gymnasium, where we could
put up at a pinch twelve or fourteen more. Our guests were received

just as they came; we were tied and bound by no rules. As long as there was room, we accepted anyone whom it seemed likely we could benefit, always giving preference to those who seemed to need help the most. We laid ourselves out especially for three classes, the sick in body, the sick in soul, and those desirous of becoming healers. No one but myself knew the names or circumstances of our inmates, so that oftentimes a man has stayed with us for six months, and no one knew who he was but myself. To most people I gave a nickname, and that avoided all difficulty. The etiquette of the house - you cannot say rules - was very simple, punctuality at meals, not to annoy any inmate unless I gave permission, when the annoyance was for the other's good, and always to be in by a quarter past ten at night. Anyone might leave when they liked even without telling me, and they might steal when they liked, if they could find anything worth stealing. The latter had its inconveniences. I remember once an invalided marine, a poor weak fellow in every respect, whom we had at last to turn out of the cubicles to sleep in the gallery, because he had so many companions that remained in the bedclothes. When I remonstrated with him for this, and suggested that the public baths and carbolic soap were a ready way of ridding oneself of such friends, he left in a huff, taking with him the plain clothes of the sailor who, out of pity, had first brought him to the house. I remember, too, Tom - we never knew his other name - a North-country boy, who had slept in almost every workhouse in England, and yet who had extraordinary reserves of good in him. When, after staying with us four months, I had arranged to emigrate him, he offered, out of kindness, to clean Mary's kitchen in the morning, but broke open her drawer and went off with £5 of house money; yet he had the grace to write from Liverpool and tell us that he had taken it; and, though we have never heard from him since, I believe some memory of S. Agatha's remaining in his mind keeps near him some idea of human, if not of divine, love. Many, many tramps like him we have sheltered, some for a few days, some for a few months. Some have turned out splendidly abroad, in the army, or as stokers in the navy. Some have gone back, for the road has a mysterious attraction that it is very hard to break them of.

Then there were the sick in body. Ah! what miracles are wrought

CHRISTMAS PARTY 1893

by a little food. We who waste so much surely never realise it. They came to us principally from London, sometimes out of the parish itself. It was not altogether the best house for invalids. Perhaps there was no more difficult task than to tell them so, and that they must go. Eating, too, is such a matter of fancy, the mind far more often than the stomach saying, "I cannot." Our common table, eating all together all the same things, was a wonderful cure for this squeamishness of appetite. But illness from starvation, and starvation because of illness, far commoner maladies than we comfortable people are willing to confess - our own meat would often choke us if we did - renders it sometimes impossible for men to eat any quantity of food, especially meat. Can you realise that? There are thousands who could not eat meat if they had it, by reason of want of use, whose digestions have become destroyed by sheer starvation. And here was the great reward in this part of our work. Whereas you could not measure the moral progress; you always could the physical. Anaemic faces growing ruddy, gloomy faces growing gay; first, perhaps, just the vegetables eaten, then a little meat as well; then the whole plate cleared. How I have rejoiced to see a little bit of bread cleaning up the plate. Then a brave attempt at a second help, and we knew the man was cured. The dear old nursery story, "Top off, half gone, all gone," and then, as a rule, his time was come, and he went.

Then the harder cases - the fellow who would really work if he could get work to do. Sometimes a footman, sometimes a clerk, sometimes a man who had been in one of the Services. Portsmouth was a bad place for this kind of fellow. There are no manufactories; every billet is in the hands of army or navy men, and I have never been able to get on with the authorities of either service.

Once, indeed, we had a great stroke of luck, when Lipton opened a shop in Portsmouth, and they allowed us to supply all the boys. That was, I suppose, five years ago, and some are there still. There is, perhaps, no sadder man in all the world than he who would and could work, and yet cannot get it. How terribly his cause is injured by the man who will never work under any circumstances! In London it was easy to deal with this class. A room opened as soon as the papers were published, a perusal of the advertisements, a hunch of bread and cheese, a cheery word of encouragement, a little perseverance in tramping on the part of the searcher, and work was generally found after a week or two. But in Portsmouth I have known them linger with us week after week. In reality the only chance was to get them away. This entailed large expenditure in advertisements, in stamps, and correspondence, until at last I have had to refuse to take in any more of these cases.

And then the most difficult cases of all - those just out of gaol, or who ought to be in gaol - each one demanding special individual care, and far more special prayer. There is no doubt that in many people stealing and drunkenness - these were the two sins we mostly dealt with - must really be looked upon as diseases. In that case the cause of the disease is the first thing to be ascertained, and that requires considerable time for true diagnosis; and here you have first to learn that all drunkards are liars, generally very successful liars, and many thieves as well. I have been taken in over and over again, and yet the only way to cure this is to make them feel that you believe in them. This in the long run shames most men into truth. I remember a lad who had tramped to us from Southampton with a most plausible story - concerning which I wrote - managing to intercept the letters, and so gaining three or four days more grace; caught in the act of stealing, so impressed with being forgiven that he told his true story, which was that he had been in gaol twice for stealing. Living with us for nine months, he became altogether changed, learning to pray, making a first confession, being confirmed, and everything was arranged for his going out to a friend of mine in America; he became so trusted that he carried all my letters to the post, and even my money to the bank ; and then on the eve of one Derby Day, seeing the fatal odds quoted, he stole a letter of mine, in which he knew there was a postal order for £1. He had the grace, after he had stolen it, to telegraph to me the fact (that sixpence the first-fruits of his robbery), for I had just left home. Surely that is a disease; and yet one knows that every resistance to temptation is a tremendous gain towards its cure. A year ago he worked his way home from America in a cattle-boat just to stay two days with me, to tell me his failures and his successes. When last I heard from him he had been going on all right since his return. How magnificent are these efforts to do right, in spite of overwhelming temptation! How infinitely more heroic than

our smug contentment at our own honesty, who have never had
cause to steal. And yet falling, in a moment, discovery, gaol, despair.
Has Christian society no better method?

I shall never forget the look on the face of Dr. Thorold one
morning when I told him that the two companions he had chosen to
sit with at supper the night before were both experienced thieves.
One had been in gaol three times, the other twice; the former a
clergyman's son, the latter one of those curious instances, in which
the lowest surroundings had not been able to obliterate outward
signs of a better heredity. We generally sat at meals according to the
order of our coming, but I thought he, being a Bishop, and
unaccustomed to our ways, had better choose his own companions. I
had only seen the lads the day before, and I watched the scene with
amusement, qualified with terror for his ring and watch. However, he
found them very pleasant, and when I told him what I knew about
them, he could hardly believe it was possible. In three or four days'
time I discovered that, as far as I was concerned, the clergyman's son
was hopeless, but for the other there was every chance, and the
diagnosis was pretty correct, for the one facilitated his departure by
stealing some money, and, though I hear from him from time to time,
he is, I think, at this present moment in gaol. The other emigrated,
got into the hands of a good man, whose daughter he married,
though I am proud to think he was honourable enough, even at the
hazard of losing his love and his prospects, to tell his father-in-law
the history of his past life.

I don't think that even when we failed altogether with a man we
were disappointed. How could we in a few months hope to set right
what many years had made wrong? But over and over again letters
have come to me, showing, at least, how our endeavours had not
been altogether in vain. Ashamed, perhaps, to come back to us,
because of the way they had treated us, they yet preserve in their
minds a remembrance of us, a little salt to prevent wholesale
corruption. To believe that someone loves me, is akin to believing
God loves me, and I know that there are many in all parts of the
world to-day whose only sight of the love of God was their sojourn
with us. One longed to be able to devote many years to such a one, to
give up all one's time. Of course, that was impossible, we had a

hundred other things to do, a hundred other people to help. People often ask. How long did you keep a man? As long as we saw that there was any hope. There is no such thing as time in dealing with cases like these. One poor Irish landlord, a perfect gentleman by birth, whom we put into a lodging, because it was not convenient to have him in the house, was with us until we left. We had had tremendous hopes of him. He began to go to church. His manhood seemed to be restored. Then in a fatal moment I allowed him to earn a little money in the town during the election. Quite old he was. And yet that pound meant drink, gambling, loss of all he had gained, then fear of us, until Conibeere discovered him almost naked and utterly broken down in health.

Of course, many have turned out splendidly. I remember one, who had been in gaol for eighteen months, coming to us as a very last resource. I remember how, day by day, we could notice the giving up of the slouch, the desire for a clean collar, for a bath, for rational talk, for intellectual books to read. And now from America he writes me letters full of the deepest interest on religious as well as secular matters, and underlying them all a modesty and a gentleness which shows him to be infinitely superior to what he was before he got into trouble.

Here is a very typical case, the last one we dealt with; perhaps someone who reads this may like to help him. I had known him sixteen years ago, for his two brothers, soldiers, were great friends of mine. He is one of the cleverest men at figures I ever knew, but he got into bad ways in London, and when the consciousness that he was a thief pressed out of him all hope, he walked down to Landport, craving to be saved. I felt at once that his repentance was only skin deep, that if I could have set him free, he would merely have gone on his way rejoicing till another temptation came. There was only one remedy, "You must give yourself up." He thought it was a hard judgment, but he was wise enough to adopt it. Alas, how selfish personal distress makes one! And so in all the agony of our last five weeks I forgot all about him. I was taking supper with my sisters about ten days before we left. We had just heard that Canon Gore was going to send a Mr. Bull to take temporary charge, when a telegram arrived, "I will be with you at 7.30 p.m." (Signed) "Bull." Though we were very grateful that Mr. Bull could conscientiously come, I think for a moment we thought the telegram a little cool. While we were discussing it, a ring at the bell, and to my delight it was my lad from gaol. I took him up to London with me when I left, and kept him and his wife for a little time with me, and now I have sent him out to his brother in America, who is going to help him. The discipline of gaol gave him the grace of amendment. Our help restored to him faith in himself, and there is no doubt that he will do well; but he cost me over £15, and as I am utterly impecunious now, he will have to pay it, which will prevent his wife rejoining him. If this burden were removed from him by somebody paying it, I need not say it would be the completion to what I believe to be his reformation.

Drink, of course, was a much more difficult thing to cure, because the physical craving is an additional temptation. Perhaps this is the reason why drink, though not more deadly in the eye of God, is more deadly in its consequences than most sins, because it not only causes that dementia, which forces men to do outrageous and monstrous things, but it injures some brain tissue, which prevents a man using his self-will, and finally destroys self-will altogether. People got to know, I suppose, that we were willing to receive clergymen and others who had gone wrong through this, and so in the last eight years there have always been one or two inebriates resident in our house. If a man really wanted to be cured, it was merely a matter of time, but many came to us persuaded by their friends, having no real desire to amend. When, too, you preach to others, it is very easy to become a castaway yourself. When you have held the Sacrament in sacrilegious hands, you have voluntarily deprived yourself of the chief power of amendment. Some of the best workers and the noblest souls become slaves of this most awful curse. It has always seemed so strange a thing to me that there is no place for a clergyman who has gone wrong. If they are condemned to seek reformation in the workhouse, it is almost impossible to hope for their amendment. The very knowledge of the height from which they have fallen, the grace that they have despised and trodden under their feet, makes them, if there is any honesty in them, hopeless of ever amending themselves, and they grow callous and hard-hearted. They have often come to me from the workhouse, from the army shelter home, from gaol. Our house was manifestly bad for this purpose. It was impossible to have sufficient supervision. Then, too, the character of the clergyman never can be wholly laid aside, and as a rule, in a few days, even though in lay attire, they were recognised by the rest of the inmates, which made it particularly difficult for them. In all other religions I think there is a home for these poor lost sheep, or a monastery, or some place; but in this country, alas! left to themselves, they go from bad to worse. I remember well one, whom his friends had promised to supply with lay clothes, arriving an hour and a half late, dressed in clericals, so drunk that all the children in the street were mobbing him, and when I suddenly opened the hall-door to see what the row was, unable to stand, he fell prone at my feet. Even when we got him to bed he declared he had had nothing to drink but some milk. A doctor, who was with me at the time, tried to persuade him he was drunk, but he utterly refused to acknowledge it. We bore with him as long as we could, and at last I had to tell him that he would have to leave by a certain date. My Low Church brethren were willing to relieve me of anyone who could flatter them that it was our High Church ways they objected to, and so with ease he borrowed eighteen shillings from one of our brethren; but when he returned at night in an hilarious mood and was refused more, he promptly smashed the windows. I saw him in the workhouse afterwards. I promised that if he would stay there for six months I would try and do something for him. He thought me very hardhearted and unkind, because I would not take him back again. Indeed I received a very amusing comment from him on the last sermon I preached at S. Agatha's, which he had read in the paper. I had been expressing to my dear people my consciousness of many hard words I had said to them, and how often I felt a want of tenderness and forgiveness on my part had marred my ministry. Commenting on this, he said, "I am quite sure it was your treatment of me in the workhouse which you had in mind when you spoke those words."

I believe there is only one hope for the drunkard, and that is teetotalism, but there are a thousand other things which he needs besides. Many of them have become drunkards through the bitterness of poverty, to have to live like gentlemen, when they had not enough income to keep body and soul together; many through the snobbishness of the vicar, who often treats the curate as if he were in no sense his equal, and is jealous of his mixing with the well-to-do people of the congregation. Few people can measure the loneness of many a curate's life, especially if he is a little on in years, so that the female part of the congregation do not admire him. Many become so because of an inward rebellion against their own work; they feel more or less that their preaching and teaching is humbug. Many become so because at certain moments, when they have no energy, no vital force, they are compelled, either in private or public, to make a great mental effort. Many become so because of the utter discomfort of their lodgings, want of proper food, etc. A drop of drink is such a swift miracle-working remedy. The higher clergy, who have never been tempted in these ways, ought to have infinite compassion for these men. There ought to be, in several centres, places managed by the most loving, hopeful people, so that, at any rate, they might have a generous chance, and the awful scandal they do to the Church might be removed. Our lay drunkards were infinitely easier to deal with than our clerical ones, and I have in my mind many, who lived with us for a little time, who are now quite free from their former temptations. You may imagine something of the burden that this kind of work entailed on me, a burden that no one could share, for I alone knew their histories, and therefore their needs.

But I do not want you to think for a moment that our house only contained inmates like this. There are many excellent men, now priests, who came to us to discover vocations, some 'Varsity men, some National schoolmasters, some shopmen. Mostly two or three like this were living with us, helping me in a hundred different ways, and learning, I think, a good deal. How hideous the question of examination, the gross unfairness of the system. For instance, the 'Varsity man can be ordained at once, if he pass the Bishop's exam. A literate, who is very likely a far more valuable man, has not a look in in most dioceses. The Bishops seem to think that a B.A. Oxford, Cambridge, or Dublin, is the very best of educations. They are always saying, "We want University men." Nobody values Oxford and Cambridge more than I do, especially their meals; there is a royal prodigality about a breakfast at Oxford that is truly magnificent. There is also in those four years of 'Varsity life a very delightful environment, a little work crammed in as an excuse for much enjoyment, much idleness. Of course, there are two exceptions to this - the man who reads, and the man who plays games, a physical and intellectual training, which, if combined, produces a really matured man. But the vast majority of men saunter their time away, excusing themselves, I suppose, because Oxford and Cambridge are holy ground. They gain a certain facility of expression, a certain ease of manner, the tone, if they are at a good college, of good society. Few take to religion, about them the less said the better; somebody whispers in my ear - I hardly like to write it - the word "smug." On the whole, it has splendid advantages, it is a time of easy growth, a time of making friendship, a time of acquiring charm. But that it is a time of acquiring character for the priesthood, hardness, endurance, mental struggle, intellectual activity, no one but a Bishop can imagine. Wonderfully did these men add to the charm of Landport.

Once I was giving a parochial retreat in Holy Week. I noticed a man with a hard, strong, strangely kindling face. When the day's work was over, painfully rubbing his knees, for he had never knelt so long before, he told me he had come from Ireland, and wanted to stay with us a little. He had been the master of an endowed school there, who had saved enough money out of his pitiful salary to take a degree in Dublin by examination. He intended to stay a week, but he stayed with me for more than two years. He is one of the strongest, noblest characters I have ever known. He would have been an invaluable priest, but, alas! he could not afford to live up in Dublin, and so could not take the Divinity Testimonial. He is now a priest in Canada, and very likely will some day be a Bishop.

You know how hard it is for men to overcome shyness, especially in speaking about religion to others, and very soon after we got to Landport I noticed one young man who always brought two or three with him. When I got to know him, I discovered that this missionary spirit was very deep down in his heart, and his one hope was that some day he might be a priest. He worked very hard, for his was a Landport shop, and the hours were late, but I promised him if he would teach himself Latin and Greek I would look upon it as a proof that he was fit for the ministry. Some two years afterwards he came to me and said, "I think, if Mr. Osborne would examine me, I could satisfy you that I have tried to learn." But even this courage and determination availed nothing with the English Episcopate. He too is now doing an excellent work as a priest in America.

Of course, there were many men who came to us with no vocations at all. Concerning that the Bishops did not seem to make any inquiry. They practically know nothing of their candidates, and yet surely this might be a valid excuse for the monstrous possession of a palace, and for an income which would enable them to keep S. Paul's rule, "to be given to hospitality." I fear it is rather the influential laity and dignified clergy on whom they exercise this virtue. I am, of course, willing to allow that great discrimination would be needed in discovering this vocation. Young men came to us with no vocations; a few were utterly vicious. One, I remember, moved with pity at my ill-health and overwork, inaugurated a collection so that I might have a holiday, kindly suggesting that the people asked to contribute should not mention the matter to me, as I might refuse it. He went for a nice holiday himself, and afterwards was aggrieved because I would not recommend him to another clergyman. But men like this are soon choked off, and the discipline of laughter in our house was particularly wholesome. The discipline of labour, too. Once I remember a man almost prostrating himself at my feet, and saying, "All I crave is a habit." It was before I sold my library, and I saw that the books were very dusty, so getting a cloth I made him clean them, and then begin a catalogue. Before a week was over, tired of the catalogue, he had fled. Oh, most blessed catalogue, what a number of vocations it has discovered as non-existent!

Many men would come because of the exaggerated account of our ritual. Matins, said plain, at 7.30 a.m., was a great stumbling-block to them, and when they discovered that our own altar-boys knew nothing about ritual, except the part that they themselves had to perform, they thought that we were strangely behindhand. One having to serve at my celebration, because the usual server was ill, screamed out in an agony after the service was over, "Oh, Father, when your hands are extended your fingers are unjoined. Could you not join them?" His ears discovered whether I could or not. And with these ritualists came many of the same character, men coquetting with Rome or with unbelief. They were utterly dumbfounded to discover it all dealt with as a matter of want of wholesome employment of body and intellect, to be recommended to try a little real activity, to find that neither Rome nor unbelief was regarded as a very terrible danger to them, but that their credulity or doubts were only another spelling of self-importance. If they were good fellows they soon fell into line again. Of course, there were exceptions to these, those with whom one watched through agonies, and in those agonies discovered prayer, and in prayer rediscovered the sight of God, souls very heavy and sick to death, of tenderest conscience, most noble, most suffering. It has been a privilege beyond all words to be to these what the Blest Three refused to be to Christ, and I for one am bold to say that, whether Romans or unbelievers to-day, a compassionate Heart understands, knows, and blesses. Many such, I think, went away comforted and strengthened, though perhaps more by the cheeriness and good fellowship of our house than by anything we were able to say.

Then, too, there were Romans desiring to become Anglicans, I fear the worst lot of all. I suppose one ought to rid oneself of one's instinctive dread of these persons, but I have met such hideous frauds amongst them. Almost my first day in Portsmouth I was persecuted by a wretched priest, whom, as soon as he had opened his mouth, I discovered to be a drunkard and a liar. He arrived one evening about five with a little bag in his hand. When I told him I was too busy to talk to him, he said, "I will leave my bag, and return at dinner-time." Then when I told him there was only dinner for two, and neither I nor my secretary would share ours with him, he said, "Oh, it does not matter; but I will return to sleep." And when I told him that there were but two bedrooms, and neither I nor my secretary would share these with him, the mask fell off his face. He had been received into the Church of England, and the Church of England was bound to support him; he would soon make it too hot for me in Portsmouth. I never stood face to face with a more hideous blackmailer, but it was not until I had opened the door and had taken him by the back of the neck that he retired.

Then came a most innocent monk, demanding rest and peace to meditate on the errors of his past religion, to discover the beauty of mine. Correspondence with his former superiors proved he was

utterly unworthy; but then there are always two sides to every
question, and one felt bound to give him a patient hearing. Those
who shared his room said he not only went prayerless to bed, but in
the same shirt he had worn during the day. This latter habit they
much objected to. Alas! in him the habit did not make the monk. But
when I discovered that Ally Sloper was his favourite reading, my
mind was more perplexed about him, and I thought that this course
of study could be as advantageously pursued at his father's, a
respectable grocer in the North of England, and so I made him the
offer of either sending him back to his monastery, or to his own
home. That day came a wonderful conversion in him, his face all
radiant with delight. He had been spirit-led, as he said, to the
Presbyterian minister's, and the minister and his wife had so
expounded religion, that he had discovered that the Church of
England was quite as false as the Church of Rome, and now peace
and happiness was reigning in his heart. Not long after the town was
covered with placards, "A monk will expose the enormities of
monasteries." The lectures, however, fell rather flat. Gossip said they
were not spicy enough; I imagined invention had failed. We used to
see him as he lived in comfort at the minister's, but he cast pitying
glances on us. Some time after the police called - they wanted
information concerning him; and a year's retirement, free of charge,
was granted him for obtaining money under false pretences. Alas!
this did not suffice to really convert him, for some time ago he got a
further term for the same thing in Ireland.

The mention of this monk's shirt reminds me of a difficulty we
often experienced, even amongst our nicest visitors. We discovered
that not merely pyjamas, but night-shirts, were the exclusive property of the upper classes; and I remember once providing these garm-
ents for all who were without them, on condition that they would
wear them every night. I had forgotten all about it until I heard one
of the boys - I think it was Tommy - say, with conscious pride, to
another, "I always wear my night-shirt." This roused my curiosity,
and, on making investigations, I discovered that he did wear it, but
over all his other clothes, except coat, waistcoat, and trousers.

I suppose there were generally fourteen of us living in the house,
besides two curates who lodged outside, because I hardly considered

it fair to compel them always to live in public, while at almost every meal there were what we call probationers. If, after watching these for a day or two, we discovered that there was a chance to really reform them, they would be taken from the lodging where they had been placed, and brought into the house. Then there were countless sailors coming to stay a day or a month, as the case might be, disappearing for two or three years, and then turning up as if they had never been away. Then the convalescent and those out of work, so that our dinner generally doubled our regular number of inmates. Can you imagine a better school for men who desired to learn their fellow men? Over it all there was a spirit of good fellowship and kindliness that seldom failed.

If a very disagreeable-looking or dirty person was intruded, and his presence forced beside some rather swell Wykehamist, or a budding cleric with conceited notions about himself, this difficulty never lasted more than for a moment. A look was always sufficient to make the objector understand the real good he would gain, even if he carried away to his personal inconvenience something from the man beside him. But sometimes the devil was let loose for a space amongst us, and everything went wrong. Boys stole from one another, men came in drunk, sometimes acts of gross insubordination occurred, when my heavy hand had to fall on the whole family. I remember once for three long days we lived on bread and cheese. We had had a very large Christmas party. Two or three days after Boxing Day, as I came into the Sunday dinner, I heard piercing shrieks from Blind Willie, - you will hear about him again, I expect. Someone had smashed up his hat, and no one would tell who had done it. As a rule boys were ready to confess, but there was a spirit of obstinacy in the house to-day, and no one would tell. In a rash moment I ordered the dinner to be carried away, - alas! being in the octave, it was a kind of repetition of the Christmas dinner, - and having pointed out the wickedness of tormenting Willie, I said there would be no more meat eaten in the house until I knew who had hurt his hat. I remember well there were two inoffensive clergymen, a member of Parliament, and a guardsman staying with us, and I have reason to believe that they secretly refreshed themselves elsewhere; but the house stood to bread and cheese rations until the Tuesday morning. It was a very sharp and bitter lesson, but it is a fairly good illustration of our universal method. Over and over again, in dealing with mean and horrid ways, we have found this one of the most effectual methods. I think that to share the consequences of sin often prevents sinners, and everyone in the house realising that the burden of punishment would fall upon the guiltless, and in some sense most heavily upon myself, was a great deterrent. Vulgarity, ill manners, or horseplay would have made a home like ours insupportable, and, I think, by degrees we all learned tenderness and forbearance one with another. I suppose this is the best test of being what is called "gentlemen." In the daytime my sitting-room, in the night-time my bedroom, dominated the whole house. At half-past five every morning I got up and called the boys who were going to work, or the sailors who had to be on board at 6.30. I had a gas stove in my bedroom, and so I could go back to bed again, and read or make sermons till six. This was a very quiet hour, too, for scolding anyone in the house who needed some special talking to. Then at seven I was in church to celebrate the Holy Communion; at 7.40 we said Morning Prayer; another Celebration at eight, which the religious men staying in the house usually attended; at 8.30 breakfast, at which everybody was supposed to be present. When I had a shorthand clerk he could take down most of my correspondence while breakfast was going on. At 9.45 convalescents in body and mind went out walking till 1 p.m., unless there was any work for them to do. Sometimes it is best to let men be idle, sometimes to force them to work. All the morning I saw people, parish people, inquisitive people, people with real troubles, people with imaginary ones; but the door was always open, and everybody came upstairs as they liked. They knew if my study door was open that they could come in; if not, they must wait till it opened. Sometimes a man wanting to learn was allowed to sit in my study to see the people who came in, unless it was something private, and to hear the advice given. One learns to be a very quick judge of character, alas! oftentimes too quick, as my conscience taught me, when each night I answered before God for every one who had visited me that day. Then at one o'clock dinner, at which everybody had to be present. As far as possible everybody except myself took exercise in the afternoon, coming in to tea at 5.30. Service in the church at

SOME OF OUR VISITORS

7.30; then clubs, gymnasium, &c., till 10 p.m.; supper and prayers and everybody in their room at 10.15 p.m. At 10.30 the door was locked, and anyone coming in had to ring my bell. Sometimes I could entrust one of my helpers to go down and open the door, but, as a rule, I tried to do it myself. I have known many men shamed out of drunkenness and loose habits by the knowledge that I should have to open the door. I do not suppose in all the world there ever was a place better adapted for acquiring a knowledge of human nature. Of course, many men took advantage of it; but even from them what an immense deal we learned, and I doubt if there was such a merry home or such happy people in the whole of England. Thank God, as a rule, there were always a good many Irishmen amongst us, and so there was ever a humorous side, even to the darkest circumstances. It was one of our rules to talk nonsense, as far as possible, at meals, and we generally brought in to dinner and tea one or two little children. There is no possibility of being dull in the presence of a little child, and in my saddest moments, when I was feeling sick to death with worry and trouble, wounded oftentimes by my own brethren, the laughter and merriment of a little child brought us back to ourselves and to God.

Men coming to stay with us had often such heroic ideas of what they would like to do, were so anxious to do people good. Of course, this is a splendid notion, but it generally prevents one doing anything at all, and I am sure I and my curates and most of my workers felt that the house and family did us much more good than we did it, and so one generally said to the man, "We don't want you to do good, we want to do you good." The woman worker amongst the poor is sometimes not a prig; alas! the man worker nearly always is. I have known men choked off the very first day of their stay by some such treatment. They want to give lectures, or to teach in night school or in Sunday School, or to get up debating societies, or cricket clubs, or to boss concerts; in fact, to do anything that means the assertion of their own cleverness or good disposition towards others. How hateful it is! I always kicked at this, sometimes kicked it. I expect these workers do infinitely more harm to themselves than they do good to others. For ten long years, day and night, there were lessons for me to learn, if I only had the grace and modesty to learn them. Even in that in which men might know more, knowledge, they are but as babes and sucklings in the presence of those whom they condescend to teach, that is, if knowledge means the knowing of things likely to be useful to the knower and to the community. In speech, too, how much we have to learn; how terse and in what few words do our dear people express themselves, while the man who wants to harangue them wraps round with innumerable words, which darken all counsels and prevent all understanding, the thought that the slum lad expresses in three or four words to the point. And as to manners, every single man in my home was a gentleman, that, if thinking for others and treating them with forbearance and tenderness and love, and striving to make them feel at home and at ease, means being gentlemen. The roughest, rudest, most ignorant lad, after a month's residence, has obtained these graces. I have seen deeds of the purest chivalry, self-sacrifice which the love of God alone can measure; I have seen the withstanding of temptation even to tears and blood; I have seen agonies borne without a word, for fear I should be vexed. I take them out of my heart, where some of them have lain for eight long years - I take them out one by one, thieves, felons, tramps, loafers, outcasts, of whom the world was not worthy, having no place for them, no home for them, no work for them. I read in their eyes a tenderness, and their hearts a compassion for me, a bearing with all my ill temper, and paying me back a hundredfold in the richest coin of truest love.

VIII.
Our Sailors.

I DARESAY, as you read this account of our house, it may have been hard for you to imagine that there was a great danger of our life becoming monotonous. If no new inmate arrived in the course of a month, it was very hard to go on inventing new jokes; and yet, in an atmosphere of discipline and of sorrow, merriment was of the first importance, and God sent this element to us in our sailor lads. The first hour I was in Portsmouth I recognized that the sailors would be our chief difficulty, our chief source of danger; but I hardly realized that they would be the cheery, breezy element, driving away cobwebs, and preventing monotony.

Naturally one's first thought was for the boys on the training-ship *St. Vincent*. First, because a good number of our parish lads had joined her; secondly, because many clergymen in different parts of the country wrote to us about individual boys; and, thirdly, because they seemed to need us most. In one sense there can be no life more wholesome or more improving than a boy's life on a training-ship; its splendid punctuality and obedience, healthy hours, sufficient food, no single idle moment, great attention as to bodily health, and, as a rule, very interesting and diversified employment.

And, over it all, a rough-and-ready give and take, which, if in certain individuals it degenerates into cruelty, is, on the whole, I think, as merciful as possible, when you consider that a thousand lads, rough and smooth, educated and ignorant, gentle and brutal, are herded together. We have sometimes come across gentlemen's sons; once, I think, a Blue-coat boy; very often sons-of well-to-do shopkeepers and superior artizans. Many of these boys suffer agonies for the first month or two, some through the whole of their course; but I remember at Harrow some boys suffered agonies all through their school-life. But take it as a whole, and for the majority of boys, I doubt if there is a better training anywhere.

Two great blots, however, there are on this system, and I cannot see how they can be amended. First, the great difficulty about religion. I have known the most excellent naval chaplains in training-ships getting hold of the boys by storm, impressing them not only at the moment of their confirmation, but, I believe, through all their future life. I know one chaplain who keeps a record of every boy who has passed through his ship, not only discovering all about him at home, but following him on through his career. He has a kind of guild, to which those who care to do so may belong, and they carry a letter of commendation to the chaplain of their next ship, and so on. If his system could only be a little extended, enormous good might be done. But such chaplains are few and far between, not because they do not desire to do all they can, but because all men have not the method of dealing with lads of this, description.

I remember one most excellent man, just appointed to the *St. Vincent*, most anxious to do all he could. In the middle of our conversation I said, "You had better come and have a cup of tea." But when, on entering the dining-room, he saw that it entailed sitting down with eight or ten of his own boys, he was anything but comfortable. An awful silence for a few moments, and then he jerked out, looking round at them with a grin, "I think this is the first time you have had the honour of taking tea with me." Why should such a man be sent to a training-ship?

The best chaplain we ever had at Portsmouth was taken away after six months, because he was a naval instructor as well, and therefore had to go to a ship where there were middies; but I am sure in the day when every man's work is tried, those six months will be the most fruitful and abiding.

If only some system could be devised by which the most suitable chaplains could be retained in the training-ships - indeed, one might go further, if it were possible, and suggest that the captain, and more especially the first-lieutenant, should be chosen for their aptitude for this kind of work, understanding the needs of boys, with a genius for discovering the methods of the instructors and the warrant-officers, the gain would be enormous. We need in England sailors perfectly

91

trained for their work. This they will never be, unless they love their work. The first eighteen months, as a rule, either creates or mars this love. If in those eighteen months there could be a little individualising, a little less treating everybody like a machine - and this can only be done by those who have daily and hourly intercourse with the boys, as instructors in the schoolroom or in their different squads - if there could be a little sympathetic compassion and understanding of them, they would turn out much more valuable men. And this practically almost altogether depends upon the first-lieutenant, and could depend, I think, a good deal upon the chaplain.

The other difficulty is the utter loss of all idea of home. There are some boys who never come ashore from week to week, and when they do go home for their leave, so unaccustomed are they to all the gentle side of what home means, all that part of it which springs from woman's influence, that they are very soon tired of it. You must realize that these lads of fourteen are far older in experience than lads of the same age in another class, and this eighteen months in their life is just the time when they turn from boys into men, the real turning-point; new passions, new powers, are developing every day. Body and intellect, both wholesomely treated, are developing with extraordinary rapidity, but the soul has hardly any opportunity of growth. And, therefore, the sailor oftentimes remains a boy, or rather a man who has never matured, if our manhood consist of soul as well as body and intellect. I think this was the thought which struck us most as the *St. Vincent* boys began to use our house more and more. And very glad we were that they should use our house, for Portsmouth is not the best place for boys to be in. Whether they land at the Hard or at the Point, there is generally temptation very near them, temptation which has a special attraction for them, because they have a special desire to play the man, and manliness in certain classes is only another word for sin. Every Thursday and Saturday, their half-holidays, and every Sunday afternoon, we opened our house freely to them. We devised all kinds of amusements, and wearied ourselves with inventing sports, which were never received with very much verve. Our great gymnasium, of course, was always a source of joy. I remember one time, when the Saint possessed the best gymnastic, football, and cricket team, I should think, in any boys' institution in the world, when Jimmy Caulfield was lieutenant, the best fellow I ever knew with lads. We gave them a football in the gymnasium, and never realized, till the house was nearly blown up with an explosion of gas, that a football was likely to smash all the burners. Then we tried singing, with somebody to play the piano, but when the accompanist had gone away, the sailors discovered that feet produced better music than hands. This emulation to play proved a great misfortune to us, for when we locked up the piano, some of them tore away the silk which covered the front of it, and broke a lot of the keys. On Sundays, too, this music led to hymn singing. I think I objected to that more than to anything else. It seems to me nothing can be more irreverent or likely to destroy religion, than the bawling out of the most sacred words and names, without one single thought as to what they mean. I myself believe that comic songs would be far less harmful. But the fittest always survives, and we discovered, what common sense might have taught us at first, that being very much employed all the rest of their time, what they really liked best was loafing, mixed with conversation, pictures, reading, and writing home.

I have been wonderfully helped in my management of these afternoons by two men, to whom the mission owes a good deal besides, William Hays and Albert Conibeere. Urged by the former of these, we made a new departure, and asked leave that boys whom we knew, or who were recommended to us, might use our house as if it were their own home, sleeping on Saturday nights. This gave us the opportunity of speaking a word privately about religion, because any boy, whom we knew on the ship, who wanted to go to Holy Communion, could do so with more hope of preparation and of quiet than he could on board. So,"Dolling's party," as the master-at-arms would call them as they left the ship, became an established fact. Once or twice this liberty has been abused. Once a lad used it as an opportunity for running away. Five or six times boys came home the worse for drink. But considering that for five years eight or nine lads used our house every Saturday night, except when away on leave, transgressors were extraordinarily few. Once I remember having to threaten to stop this party altogether because two boys got drunk, and we had the most piteous and abject apologies from a large number of them. As a rule, every boy had to be in at a quarter-past ten. Most of them spent all the evening in the gymnasium. If they asked leave, however, they might go to the theatre, or if they had any special friends in the town, whom I approved of, they might be a little later. Latterly those coming have been chosen by Conibeere. He kept a book in which all the boys' antecedents were written down, the number of visits each had paid us, whether he was a Communicant, etc. The boys spending the afternoon could tell Conibeere who wanted to come, and privately whether they wanted to go to the Holy Communion. Thus I always got a chance of saying a word of advice and a word of prayer with each one, but we were most careful never to press religion, or show more hospitality to the religious; if anything we erred, perhaps, on the other side. There can be no greater danger than making religion pay, a danger, I think, into which those who manage Soldiers' and Sailors' Institutions are most prone to fall - a danger which often leads sailors, at any rate, into a fear of making friends with the chaplain, or of going to Communion, lest their mates should misjudge them as being crawlers or hypocrites. It is wonderful, for instance, how popular teetotalism becomes if some officer is specially interested in it, or how well a Bible Class is attended if patronised by some one in authority. This oftentimes is a great stumbling-block to the modest man, who is really religious, and yet is afraid of his religion being misunderstood by his mates.

And if you ask me about the after results of all this labour, I am afraid I can say very little. Sailors seldom, or never, write. I have known lads use our house continually for eighteen months, then be ordered abroad, and walk in in three years' time, saying, "Oh, I lost your address," or "I didn't know what to say, so didn't write." And then they would use the house again as if they had only left it yesterday, very likely showing us that they had thought about us by bringing us some impossible gifts - "curios" they would call them - sometimes a monkey, sometimes a bird; oftentimes astonishing me by coming into my study on Saturday night, and talking about their Communion the next day, with a wonderful, simple story of their difficulties, perhaps of their sins. And yet, in spite of all their temptations, there was a remembrance of God, which I believe at any rate they had partly learned from us. But, dear friend, surely all statistics are abominable, and especially religious statistics, so I prefer to give none.

Of course, amongst the older sailors we could hope to do very little, unless they actually lived in the parish. They are very much a race by themselves, and don't mix well with civilians, and, as we had neither men nor plant, we dared not in any way add to our responsibilities by opening a Home for them, though I doubt if there is any disgrace for which the Church of England deserves to suffer more than the fact that there is no Church of England Sailors' Home in Portsmouth. One would think that shame, if no higher motive, would compel her to try and do her duty towards her sailors. But if she fails, there is one name that ought never to be mentioned without thanksgiving to Almighty God for her unceasing labour, and her truest and tenderest devotion to Jack ashore or afloat, the name of Agnes Weston. Her Home, close to my own parish, is worked on the most admirable lines in all secular matters, excellent food and sleeping accommodation, and, above all, personal kindness and sympathy. She has, too, a very bold and broad view of many measures by which the Service could be benefited, and a very able and willing tongue to express them either in public or in private, at drawing-room meetings or before a Committee of the House of Commons. Perhaps there is no one in England to whom the nation owes a deeper debt of gratitude, for a real elevation on the part of a most important factor in the nation's welfare and prosperity, than to Miss Weston.

And if there is any man who needs such a resting-place, and especially in the good town of Portsmouth, it is the sailor. Quiet as it may seem in the daytime, there are few worse streets at night in the whole world than Queen Street, Portsea. I am sure there are no courts in the world worse than those which crowd around it. I am sure there are no characters worse than those which infest it. If the Admiralty will only gather statistics from our Naval Hospitals as to the health of our sailors, and put themselves in correspondence with the authorities of Chatham, Plymouth, and Portsmouth, I am sure a tremendous reformation could be effected. The Admiralty and the municipalities, working together, could bring great influence to bear upon the licensing magistrates as to the number of public-houses, and their character, and upon the police authorities to vigorously put in motion the existing law as regards common decency in the streets. Why, because you have gathered into one place a large number of young, unmarried men, specially prone to temptation by the very manner of their life, should almost every house in a neighbourhood which they are bound to pass through, offer temptation? If England has no nobler incentive for this reformation, her own safety, depending upon the health of her sailors, might, at any rate, move and compel her. I am conscious that these words may wound many of my friends in Portsmouth, but I cannot refrain from writing them.

I have said that the sailor often remains a boy. There is no greater proof of this than the imprudent manner in which very often he marries; often when he has known the girl only a very few weeks, and has no knowledge of her antecedents, hardly of her disposition. Sometimes I have even known sailors marry those whom they knew had been bad characters. And if you ask him the reason, "Oh! the girl was unhappy; I thought I would make a home for her"; or, "I was afraid she might go wrong"; or even, "I wanted someone to leave my half-pay with." Marriages made like this, as you may guess, do not always turn out happily, sometimes not well; especially as the man is often away three years at a time. For, after all, the half-pay is too often very little - seven and sixpence or ten shillings a week, paid monthly, the first payment seldom being received before he has been away two months, which means that the poor girl gets into frightful debt before she receives anything. I believe that in the Mercantile Marine a woman can always get an advance note cashed. I trace back many grievous misunderstandings between husbands and wives, many children in semi-starvation, the first downward step in pawning, borrowing money at usurious rates, getting into such difficulties that only the most hateful remedy, which I dare not mention here, was possible, all to this difficulty of payment. Then, too, the sum, when received, is, if the woman has children, utterly inadequate. Surely the nation is bound to see that it is not so. It is for her sake that the sailor's wife and children are separated from the husband, that he has to keep a kind of dual establishment. And believe me, the nation cannot get rid of the responsibility by saying he ought not to have married. It is for your sake he is separated from his wife and family. It is for your sake that they are in poverty. I don't write these words lightly or inadvisedly. I have seen, over and over again, homes without food, children without clothes, wives without hope. I have come in more than once just in time to stop the wife earning money by the only method open to her.

And if the wife cries out and shames you, the widow of the sailor is, without exception, the greatest of England's disgraces. Even when the nation's pity becomes universal, and money flows in like water, as in the case of the *Victoria*, the charity of the nation is strangled by the red tape of an Official Commission. I myself prevented starvation in more than one house which should have been sacred to England, and I believe that if it had not been for Miss Weston, many would actually have died of starvation. The cruelty of the methods - they were actually contemplating using the police to make investigations; the tardiness of the relief given - they made Miss Weston's generosity an excuse, and the niggardliness of the pittance to be doled out, until public opinion forced them to increase it, should create a national scandal. The Commission has over and over again received money for a certain purpose, and not used it, but rather hoarded it up. I thank God I have been summoned to give evidence before a Parliamentary Commission, now enquiring into this soulless corporation, bereft of all bowels of compassion. The enormous sum of money given to its charge for providing for the wives and others dependent on old Crimean warriors is so tied up, that although at the death of every present pensioner there will be a surplus of over £70,000, yet countless widows of Crimean soldiers, and Crimean soldiers themselves, are living and dying in the workhouse; and though, some years ago, a sum of over £7000 was released from its original trust, and they were enabled to apply this in pensions for sailors and soldiers who died in active service, or in consequence of wounds or illness incurred in active service, they have never discovered one pensioner yet, though I suppose the *Edgar* disaster was known to every man and woman in England except the Commissioners. What one hopes to see is the creation of a new trust, which, by means of humane and competent Christian persons, should discover anyone who is entitled, by the death of a relative, to help from any special fund. When these have been liberally dealt with, the surplus should be the nucleus of a great pension fund for all sailors and soldiers. From the liberality with which appeals for the *Victoria* disaster were responded to, I have no doubt that the heart of England is perfectly sound on this question. Above all, let humane Christian hearts be the channels through which England's generosity pays back her debt to those who suffer so gallantly for her sake.

And yet happy is the widow of the man who died in the *Victoria*, in comparison with the widow of him who dies while freeing slaves in Africa, or falls overboard when, in a storm, he is performing some delicate work. There is literally no provision for her. His mates will buy his poor kit for four times its worth, will put the same object up for auction over and over again until it has reached a fabulous value, will tax themselves beyond all justice in order to send home money to the widow. But the nation will let his children be vagabonds, and beg their bread. Yea, they may even seek it in desolate places, until the extortioner consumes all that he hath, and the stranger spoil his labours. And that because he gave himself for England's peace and for England's glory. Only three months ago a young fellow died on one of the ships in the Mediterranean. His mates knew that he was going to marry a girl when he came home, and that he had already had a child by her. They collected privately amongst themselves over £40, which they sent me. I have said sailors are like boys. God bless them for their youthfulness of heart, full of generosity, and full of the tenderest sympathy and most delicate understanding for every sorrow and for every pain.

At the present moment we are going to expend many millions on building new ships. We may need them. But we certainly do need a great deal more - a great increase in every branch of the Service, especially amongst the stokers. I doubt if at this present moment we can man the ships we have. A very excellent attempt has been made in the direction of such increase in the case of the *Northampton*. Many of my own lads have been on her, and so I can speak with authority of a most splendid experiment. It takes in the lad who did not quite come up to the necessary chest measurement at the proper age, or who was suffering from some superficial complaint now cured, or whose parents were an invincible obstacle, and yet who

OUR SAILORS

always wanted to become a sailor. I believe the shorter training they get on board, because of their increased age, fits them for their work very nearly as well as the longer training. Let us have two *Northamptons*, then three, then four. You will easily find recruits. Then roll away the reproach from our Dockyard towns; remove, as far as you can, temptation from the younger sailor's life; give him a reasonable chance of promotion, and treat all branches equally. The time is coming when the stoker and engineer will be the chief men on board. The sooner this is recognised on the quarter-deck, as well as on the main deck, the better. Show him he can give adequate support to his wife and family, and that, if he dies, the nation will not forget her; and I do not think you need have any fear at all about being able to man the biggest fleet the Jingoes may desire to build. The smell of the sea is the atmosphere in which Englishmen live. The enthusiasm of travel, the spirit of enterprise, the unknown with its dangers, has a strange attraction for every Englishman, and no life supplies this as well as the sailor's life.

Very difficult though it was for them, many officers have helped us very considerably. One, now a lieutenant in China, and another, a lieutenant of Marines, will always be held by me in grateful remembrance for their help amongst our most difficult class of boys. But, of course, in a house like ours, it was very difficult for officers to feel exactly at home, for they would very likely have to share meals with men on board their own ships, and though snobbishness hardly exists among naval officers, there was a very great practical difficulty created by necessary discipline.

IX.
Our Saints.

THE sight of true heroism is the best incentive to learn to be
heroic oneself, a virtue, as you may guess, greatly needed in a house
like ours. The heroism of the soldier who dies on the battle-field is as
nothing compared with the true heroism of one who endures long
agonies of pain and suffering without murmur, who prays in the
morning, "Oh, that it were evening," and in the evening, "Oh, that it
were morning." Oftentimes it is this sight which is the only witness
for God in the lives of the poor. "It is expedient that one man die for
the people." And God granted to us, during several years of our work,
this sight of a living death. His father had been a staff-sergeant in the
army, but his mother had married again into great poverty and
distress. He had struggled as a tram-conductor as long as there was
breath in his body, and then crawled into a wretched bed in a
wretched room, shared with other members of his family, to die
without one single comfort, one alleviation of all his intolerable pain.
But even this loneness in the midst of his own was forbidden him,
and impatiently he was told to go to the workhouse to die. I shall
never forget his look of thankfulness, when I said, "If you don't mind
the noise and racket of our house, come and die with us." And as he
crossed our threshold the spirit of peace came with him; and I think
it has never altogether passed away. The good food and wine, and
better medical attendance, above all, the loving unceasing attention
of Mary, our housekeeper, brought him back again from the grave.
He lived altogether six years with us, every summer strengthening
into a little activity of body, tending our little garden across the
street, sometimes almost crawling there on his hands and knees. The
very flowers seemed to know him; they have never grown so
luxuriantly since. Surely flowers recognise love more quickly than

men, and respond to it more truly. But then the whole house was his garden, and so gently, and wisely, and lovingly did he treat the roughest and most degraded, that they all seemed to respond to the magic of his touch. Oftentimes, when the whole house was in bed, he would crawl down from his room to tell me of someone's trouble which his love had discovered. Through all the winter he was in agonies of pain, dreading every breath, and yet welcoming each breath lest he should suffocate; above all things utterly unconscious of his own influence, until the day of his death bewailing the expense and trouble that he was to others, never measuring that in a true and real sense he was God's angel of peace dwelling amongst us, for it often seemed to us as if one single breath would have carried him to that resting-place which he needed so grievously. No pleasure was so great in those hours of agony, when he could not speak or move, as to know that some poor obstinate, hopeless one, was learning the only lesson his dull soul could learn by watching his pain. So trusted was he that everyone in all the house gave their money into his care, not only the boys, but myself as well, for he kept all the Parish Collections, until they were large enough to go down to the bank. No one would have dared to have stolen from him. And then when the end was very near, and the last Sacrament had been received, he asked to be left alone. After a quarter of an hour or so I opened, as silently as I could, the door, and found him kneeling beside his bed praying as I thought his last prayer; but he had learned that divinest of all secrets, that prayer must perfect itself in service, and so his poor death-chilled hands had gathered each one's little money into its own heap, lest he should even seem to have been unfaithful. As we carried him through the streets to the church the night before his funeral, there was not a dry eye in all the parish. All the next morning when the Masses for his repose were being said, the church was crowded as on a Sunday, factory girls and Dockyardmen giving up their day's work. His memory was perpetuated in the new church by the beautifying of the little altar, which in the old church he had loved so well, for the people had collected over £14 for that purpose. Ah! would that Bishop Thorold had lived only two months longer, for his eyes filled with tears, and his heart, so long a parish priest's, could realise exactly the importance of such a memory.

Shall I tell you of another of our saints? If some ten years ago you had passed down the Hard at Portsmouth, you would have seen William Dore, a mudlark, searching for pennies in the filthy mud of the harbour for the amusement of good-natured stupids, who throw them to such-like boys. Thus he earned the pennies which were eagerly taken from him when he gained his home. He was what our boys would call a little "off," else he would not have been so imposed on by a wretched step-father. The mother, blind and paralysed, lying on a few rags in a corner of the room, strove to put some thoughts of decency into two wayward girls - one older and one younger than Willie - earning, as girls do in that part of Portsmouth, sometimes a shilling or sixpence a night, and yet with a curious pathos striving to keep from the blind mother the knowledge of how it was earned. There is a court near called White's Row, the most disgraceful place in that most disgraceful part of the town; but it is redeemed by a little chapel belonging to the mother church of Holy Trinity, where Mr. Marriott, I think, first, and afterwards Mr. Lloyd, attracted Willie. He was one of those extraordinary natures in whom religion seems to come spontaneously; for they had hardly taught him one fact when he seemed to have grasped the whole of religion. The first consequence was that he must leave his home. He had become too old to be a mudlark. The only other living open to him was a kind of hanging about and picking up odd sixpences from people whom he knew, money which was gained by sin. Then the mother died, so he came to us altogether. Whether it was inherited from her, or due to the awful exposure of his early years, the nerves of his eyes weakened, and he too became blind. But I think the pathos of his blindness was almost as great an influence for good as Boss's more apparent suffering. His one idea, to give amusement, was his method of repaying the little we did for him, and so he would learn comic songs, and sing them after dinner. Often when he knew I was troubled, I would hear his tap at the door, for he could find his way everywhere about the house, and he would say, "I think I could make you laugh if you would let me sing"; and then he would put his hands upon your head, just as a little child would do, and say, "Your head is better now." It is such faith that works miracles of healing to-day. Sometimes strange boys in the house, who did not know him, would gibe at him, or, with the horrid cruelty of boys, because he was blind, push or pinch him. Then a burst of ungoverned temper, and then an equal terror of remorse. I have found him oftentimes lying on the floor in front of the altar, having groped his way into church in penitence for these sins. His one desire, to do something for the Mission, was gratified by allowing him to become organ-blower, though, indeed, it was an arrangement open to objection, especially when there were strangers in the church. He sat in a place in which everybody saw him, and his poor blind eyes staring into the unknown, and his thick-lipped mouth forming all manner of grimace as he sang, moved people almost to laughter. We never knew how he learned psalms and hymns and chants. I have thought myself that some angel must have taught him. During catechising, too, when all the rest of the school had failed, Willie could nearly always give the correct answer. God did not will that he should die with us, for at last the doctor said that he must go to the imbecile ward in the union. The day before he died, coming out of a trance of many hours, he said, "Give my love to the Sunday School children; tell them I have answered every question," and then drawing my head quite close down to his mouth, "You will wear the black cope at my funeral."

"There is a little boy just come into Alfred Street," the district visitor said one day. "He is fourteen, but he looks like a child of five, and lives and sleeps in a little perambulator. There is no one to look after him, for his mother is in a lunatic asylum, and his father goes out at six in the morning, and does not come back till night." And so exactly I found him, our dear little Harry, all alone in this dark room in his perambulator, and on a little shelf, which his poor twisted hands could reach, his cold and wretched meals apportioned for the day. At first when we brought him to the house he was very timid and very nervous, but he soon brightened up. He never really lived with us, for his father loved him so dearly that he had to go home at night to be with him, but he was with us all day, and his little tender thread was soon woven into the woof of our common life, and on all our rough people his influence was as the influence of a little child. Sometimes, when all else fails, the roughest beasts are led by a little child. His face would wince with pain, when any boy spoke harshly to another, and I have come in and found him almost in an agony of

fear, when some rough horse-play was going on amongst them. I am
sure Dr. Fearon will never forget wheeling him in his little
perambulator up to the altar, to be confirmed by the Bishop. I do not
think I have ever seen such devotion to the Blessed Sacrament as in
that little soul. In it he saw not only Jesus, but our Father, and even
heaven as well. Strange, wonderful stories he told me of what he had
seen there, for sometimes he would doze all day by the fire in the
dining-room, in my study, or in Mary's kitchen, and then only say, "I
was dreaming of the Blessed Sacrament. Do you think someone
would wheel me to Mass to-morrow morning?" I remember so well
kissing away the last tears I saw in his eyes, as he held up in his little
shrunken hands some woollen slippers, which he had made for me, a
little secret for my birthday, and found that there was not work
enough done, and then fell back saying, "I shall never live to finish
them," and died that night.

These were but a few of the saints who have influenced our home.
But out in the parish there were just as saintly lives lived, women's
lives, so we could not bring them in to die with us. Moore's Square is
the most unhealthy spot in our district. It has never been free from
typhoid fever since I went there, and it is no wonder, for there are
slaughterhouses all round it. All of the houses are poor and squalid,
and more or less out of repair. Martha lived in the Square. Her
husband was a rough sailor, who coasted about. Often away from
home he would get converted, and clergymen would write to me
about him, but he generally signalled his return with an outburst of
drunkenness. More than once I have known all the furniture broken
up, and once her arm badly burnt, because a lighted paraffin lamp
had been knocked down. She had never heard anything about
religion, till she came into church by chance one day and heard me
preaching about the Blessed Sacrament. Very often our sermons
consisted of saying the same thing over and over again, and this day I
was speaking of the Sacrament as "the Blood of God." I must have
said the words very often, for she came round to my house that night
to ask me if it was really true that God had shed His very Blood for
her. It was a revelation to her of a love so pure and so true, a love that
had forced the Eternal out of compassion for us to take to Himself
Blood that he might shed it for our sakes. She could neither read nor

write, and as she was suffering from cancer, she had not much time to learn. Once she was operated on, and as she went off under the chloroform she whispered to me, "God's Blood." But it soon began to grow again, and day by day we could see her bodily strength decaying; such horrid decay. When you read the lives of the Saints you think that kissing the sores of the lepers is an exaggeration, but it is being done continually by the poor for the poor. Their rough hands are soothed to tenderest nursing, and their rude, vulgar, boisterous ways taught true refinement by the compassion which they feel. Hers was a very tedious case, and neighbours have children of their own, and cannot watch all day, though oftentimes all night, and so the little daughter of twelve, who would rather have been playing than tending her mother, was tied to the table. One day a neighbour, hearing cries, ran in, and the child explained, "Mother is silly: she is crying for the Blood of God." How grateful I was that the Blessed Sacrament was reserved that day! It was in truth her "viaticum."

We could never make out why, however ill she was, an old woman - Maria I will call her - would never allow us to go up to her bedroom. She was always huddled up in a little chair, covered with a thin old shawl; sometimes one doubted whether there was anything beneath it. She was quite a lady, with a beautiful pinched face, bright cheerful eyes, yet so sunken that the light was as stars seen from a well. So gracious, always doing the honours of her little home, and yet so reticent about the room upstairs; till one day suddenly taken ill at night, a neighbour discovered she had no bed - had not had one for many years. She had kept a little school, and many of the women round had been her pupils; she could not bear that they should know she needed, else they would stint themselves for her, I shall never forget how she kissed my hands the first time I saw her in the bed we got for her, and said, "I pray God you may never be as thankful for a bed as I am for this." And then, after a little while, when we passed by, she would not let us in, saying, "I can go to church and hear you, so I won't trouble you to-day. I know you are very busy." And the same thing to the district visitors, till my sister Geraldine, who, because she is the shortest, is the bravest of us all, found the bed was pawned. The poor old lady held down her head, and looked so ashamed, and would not talk about it, till a man across the street cried out, "That d-----d ruffian of a grandson came out of gaol the other day, and has pawned it." Not only did he pawn the bed, but, by his badness, he drove her to such sorrow that she lost all hope; her old body could bear no more, and, falling downstairs, she was wounded past recovery. The neighbours called in the police, but the old woman's last words were - "He did not push me." But though the coroner and jury acquitted him, the neighbours look askance at him to-day.

Many cases like this forced upon me the need of some kind of alms-houses, where I could put old ladies whose only other home was the workhouse. And so we turned the cottages standing on the intended site of the new church into homes for five or six old ladies, and when these had to be pulled down we bought other ones, so that the Mission possesses to-day twelve houses, in which five old couples and nine or ten old ladies live. It has been a part of our work most blessed; and as I have never been able to get away, owing to stress of work, for the last five years, and people have kindly given me money for my holidays, this holiday money has bought most of the almshouses. Dear old ladies, I wonder if they miss me to-day as much as I miss them. I believe the purest happiness I have ever had in all my whole life is knowing and seeing their happiness. The houses are all freehold, and the old souls pay sixpence or a shilling a week, so there is enough to pay taxes and repairs, sometimes even a balance over. Granny is not always honoured in England as she is in Germany; she does not always get the warmest seat by the fire, or the first helping from the dish; she is sometimes the drudge of the whole family; minding the baby and the little children; even when her head is splitting, the children with that shrill voice which discovers every aching nerve, cry, "It is only granny, she does not matter." Sometimes, when the house is full, she is put in the corner, where, in the days far gone, she used to put that strong, stalwart man, who now does not take the trouble to defend her.

Thank God, the workhouse is far more humane to-day in England than it was, but the remembrance of what it was, has left a feeling, a sentiment, if you like to call it so, which renders it abhorrent to every honest and earnest man and woman. I pray God the time is coming when we shall recognise out-door relief a great deal more. The

Portsmouth Guardians were wonderfully good in this respect; they tried to keep people out of the house by allowing out-door relief. And I cannot speak in too high praise of the parish doctor, Mr. Colt, and our two relieving officers, Mr. Gardiner and Mr. Vine. There is no man more admirable than the conscientious poor-law doctor. Think of attending people who never obey any of your directions, who take your medicine three doses at a time, and then come for more, who send for you continually. And though our Union was, I think, as good as most - I was on the Board of Guardians for a considerable time - I wonder whether any of us Guardians would desire to go into it ourselves. Thank God we have now four or five lady Guardians in Portsmouth, who will do for the women and children what we never could do. I remember discovering after weeks of visiting in the schools, hideous and horrid things that a woman's eye would have seen at once. I had to see three girls who were going out to service. I noticed they used their aprons instead of their pocket-handkerchiefs, and when I made enquiries, thinking this would be an obstacle to their becoming servants, they told me that they were only allowed pocket-handkerchiefs one day in the year, when they went out for their annual treat. One day at four o'clock I found them all at tea, and floating on the top of the liquid so called were lumps of grease and fat. I discovered that they had eaten their dinner of soup at one o'clock, and that tea was being served in the same porringer. A little lad broke his arm on a Saturday, and though he was bathed and dressed by the attendants, it was not known till the Tuesday. Indeed, the whole system of the schools was wrong. They ought to have been in the country, miles away from the main house. Better still, the children ought to have been boarded out. I doubt if any institutions for children are right, but I have no doubt at all that our present barrack-system is altogether inhuman and scandalous. And the same thing might be said of the Infirmary, in which there were several hundred patients, and only one trained nurse to look after them. The very sick and dying were left to the tender mercies of any old porter who had wit enough to gain a few extra pence by becoming a wardsman or wardswoman. Difficult surgical cases were nursed by these utterly inefficient persons; people were left to die alone, without anyone to moisten their lips. I am very proud to think that

OUR TENANTS

this has been mended now, and that there are certified nurses, though, perhaps, not yet a sufficient number.

The real difficulty of the whole workhouse system consists in the want of classification. There are numbers of people who spend their lives in workhouses, going from one to another. In many cases the Union is actually a premium on idleness. You and I cannot imagine a man who could like this sort of life, but such people will remain with us, until there is some system of registration, some method by which those, who are just entering on the life, may be checked and stopped at the critical moment, when a helping hand would prevent them becoming casuals. Above all we must separate from these loafers those who are forced in old age to go into the workhouse. A great deal, I know, is being done, but it is all being done in an institutional way, without any individualising, without any humanity. If there is one place in the world where the miserable divisions amongst Christian people are most manifest, it is in the workhouse. It is this, I am sure, that prevents it being worked on a Christian method. The Church of England would be jealous if it were done by Dissenters, the Dissenters equally jealous if it were done by the Church of England. So long as this ministering to the poor, which is the highest and most Christ-like of all Christian duties, is done by officials, it cannot ever be done in a Christian way to any extent, though I know, of course, there are many exceptions. And however desirous the officials are under present circumstances, there rises the question of the rates, rates managed by Guardians, who are often recklessly extravagant in all the outward part of their organisation, which is seen by the public, and shockingly mean as regards the small expenditure which makes all the difference between comfort and discomfort.

Honestly, one's deepest disappointment about the working man, is his utter want of interest and understanding at all times of municipal and other elections. The new method of electing Guardians may alter this, but I very much doubt it. I suppose it is wrong to be impatient with people only recently enfranchised, and, perhaps, not yet understanding their responsibilities; but surely it is the part of the clergy to preach, in season and out of season, the grave duty of every man who has a vote for an office in the town in which he lives, that every man must recognise that God will hold him responsible for that vote, and that, if he gives it wrongly, it will be no excuse that his political club, or the kindly Primrose lady, advised him so to give it. I am very grateful indeed for the experience I gained both on the Board of Guardians and on the School Board. It brought me in contact with many men of very different opinions to my own, who treated me with great kindness and consideration, and for the majority of whom I entertain a very deep and true respect. But sometimes I could not help feeling that on the School Board we were not all educationalists, and on the Board of Guardians some were rather the guardians of the rates than the guardians of the poor. Above all, the expenses of management and the creation of plant were altogether out of proportion to the amount expended on the objects which we had in view. I venture to hope that the day is not far distant when that fetish of red tape, which strangles almost all English enthusiasm, will cease to dominate us, and when simple Christian common sense will become the method by which, at any rate, two of the most important of our duties, the educating of our children and the caring for our poor, are carried out. But it will not be done until electors choose the best man for either post - the only consideration being to get the best man - and we rid ourselves of that hateful thought that everyone desires some gain, either for himself, or for the church or party to which he belongs, by taking office.

And surely, if every citizen has his municipal duty, he has an imperial duty as well. I know that many people were very displeased with me, because I took what is called an active part in politics. Does a doctor or a lawyer cease to be a politician because he has got clients? Why then should a clergyman, because he has got parishioners? I quite hold that it would be wrong for him to canvass or to influence his people privately as to their votes; but I believe, on the other hand, that if he is conscious that he has anything to say worth saying on the question of politics, or that might help his neighbours to form a truer, better, or nobler judgment on these questions, it is his bounden duty to say it. This was a policy I always endeavoured to pursue. I never once asked a single person to vote my way, but I did, when opportunity occurred, go upon the platform and tell people what my opinions were, and I am not the least ashamed of having done so.

X.
Our Battles Civil.

IF I have ventured, in the last chapter, to speak of the duty which everyone owes to the town in which he lives, I fear that, for several years of my work in Portsmouth, I was very oblivious of this duty. The labour and watchfulness needed to try and cleanse our own little district made one forget the larger, but less apparent, duty. Indeed, many of my brethren felt that I had rendered their work more difficult, by uprooting dangers from my own district which located themselves in theirs. There is much, of course, to be said for this line of thought, but self-preservation is one's first instinct, and if, in preserving myself and my own children, I have wronged others, I am sorry for it. But I do not think that I had ever let one day pass, in Portsmouth, without praying that I might realise the grave responsibility which rested on every inhabitant, and I believed especially on the clergy. I had tried, in preaching to men alone on Sunday afternoons, to speak out quite plainly on these social subjects, and this had brought me into contact with most of the labour leaders. For a long time all labour reform, in Portsmouth, was a great difficulty, for the Dockyard did not welcome its workers joining Trade Societies. However, thank God, that reproach has all been rolled away, and I believe myself the day is not far distant when employers will find that the men's Unions are really a great gain in the solution of the whole Labour Question. Everything that tends to make the working man more intelligent and more self-reliant, is a tremendous gain, and there is no doubt that the better hours which men work, and the better wages, have this tendency. Of course, there are two dangers - first, as the Unions grew stronger, they had a tendency to look at all questions merely from the workman's point of view, and, secondly, there was a danger of the individual wasting his increased wages and leisure in bad ways. In all acts of emancipation the first enjoyment of liberty may turn to licence, but such licence never lasts very long, and, I think, looking back over the last thirty years' history of the Labour Question in England, one might say that this licence has almost never existed. At any rate, I was continually struck with the enthusiasm for righteousness that I discovered amongst the majority of the leading working men with whom I was brought in contact. I saw how keenly they recognised that though the creation of character was the chief thing to be aimed at, yet the creation of character, amidst temptations touching one at every single moment, added enormous difficulties to the education of every right-minded young man and woman. A great deal of cant has been talked about what is called the "Nonconformist Conscience," and I am quite willing to believe that many of those most *en evidence*, have, by their want of tact, and, I would add, want of true understanding of the working man, prejudiced the British public. But I can testify to this fact, that every word I uttered in Portsmouth on these subjects, was, in a large measure, but the echo of earnest words said to me, and prayers prayed with me, by working men, who were almost always, I say it with shame as a priest of the Church of England, Nonconformists. Why are these men not in communion with our Church? Surely that is the most important question for those in authority in the Church to ask themselves. The answer is not a difficult one. For their fathers and for themselves the Church of England has practically forbidden all work. They are trained in their own denominations to be class-leaders, itinerant preachers, to visit the sick, often to govern the chapel as elders. They are on a perfect equality with their minister, they tell him plainly what they think about him, and the needs of the men amongst whom they live. In years gone by their forbears suffered for what they held to be the truth; the remembrance of that suffering is bred in the bone of the children. But for all those who are interested in the Labour Question, there can be no thought so full of thankfulness to God, and of hope for the future, as the knowledge that the vast majority of labour leaders are deeply religious men.

For a long time I had been trying to organise the shop-assistants in the town. Would you believe it that, even now, Portsmouth has no weekly half-holiday, no early closing? The vast majority of the better shops, in our part of the town, do not close till 7.30 the first four nights in the week, on Fridays at 10, on Saturdays at midnight. The little shops never seem to close at all, day or night. There is something particularly pitiful in the class of shop-assistants. As a rule they will not help themselves. There is very little esprit amongst them, and a great deal of snobbishness. If some went on strike, their places would be filled within twenty-four hours, and one class will not mix with another. If you will not help yourself, God cannot help you, far less man. So, practically, one was fighting an impossible battle, for one or two large shopkeepers stood in the way of all reform. In the middle of the agitation, to my utter astonishment, I was told that the new minister of the Lake Road Baptist Chapel, Mr. Joseph, would be very glad to come and see me about it. I knew many of the Nonconformist ministers in the town were in sympathy with me, for several of them had written to me, when I resigned, in 1890, to say how sorry they were, and how they earnestly prayed that I would not leave Portsmouth. I felt that if Mr. Joseph was willing to stand by me, not only on the platform of shop-assistants, but with regard to the drink question too, I had indeed gained a most important ally. The congregation at Lake Road has more men in it than any church in Portsmouth - surely that is the best test of a Christian Church - and I knew that their minister was a true representative of his congregation. After many talks with him and some of his brethren, there was no doubt at all left in our minds that the Drink Question lay at the root of every evil in Portsmouth. With a population of 159,255 we had 1040 licences, or one licence to 153 people; or, deducting infants and total abstainers, 25 per cent, of the population, one licence for every 115 people. This is enormously above the average of almost all the large towns in England, the great seaport towns, or even the other Dockyard towns. In several Bills for the revision of the Licensing Question, submitted to Parliament, it has been proposed that licences should be granted in towns in the ratio of one per thousand; that would mean the reduction of licences, in Portsmouth, from one thousand and forty to one hundred and sixty.

I have no quarrel with the publican. I have known many of them to be the most respectable people, whose righteous souls were vexed, day by day, by the circumstances under which they and their children were forced to live; and yet, because they had invested their little all in a public-house, they had no other chance of a livelihood. In Portsmouth, too, the publican seems to suffer far more than in other towns, for the transfers are much more frequent - that is, a man invests his savings in a public-house, finds it does not pay, and has oftentimes to leave it, realising very little of the money which he put into it. Almost all the houses in Portsmouth are tied houses - that is, the publican has to sell, exclusively, the beer of the brewer who owns the house; and if he does not sell a sufficient quantity he is soon reminded of it, for the brewer's profit is far more largely made out of the profits from the beer than from the rent of the house. There is only a certain amount of legitimate drinking in any town - that is, drinking because a man actually needs the drink. If the drinking were limited to this, an enormous number of houses would close without any interference of the magistrate. And so the publican has to do all sorts and kinds of things to induce men to stay in his house and drink. Everyone knows that there are innumerable ways of adulterating or faking up drink; that, if gambling and betting are allowed, men will congregate; that, if bad characters fill the bar, certain men will stay there; that, if the singing of vulgar songs is allowed, it is a great attraction, and makes men who roar the choruses all the more thirsty. Many publicans, of course, are too high-minded to employ these methods; but many who see starvation facing themselves and their children, do use them. Needs must when the devil drives; and certainly, in this case, the devil is the driver. Then it is very hard to refuse drink to a man who has already had too much, not only because you lose the price of the glass, but very likely his custom, as well as his friends'. However diligent and efficient the police are, it is utterly impossible for them to see that every public-house is conducted on legitimate lines. A large public-house, with a big trade and hardly any seats, where people take their drink and go out again, does, comparatively speaking, little harm. In towns with slums like Portsmouth, nearly all the harm is done by the little public-house. And these little houses are not scattered over the whole town; they are gathered, as a rule, into little districts. In Portsmouth proper, for instance, with a population of 6938, there are 75 public-houses; in Portsea, with a population of 15,260, there are 145. And these are really the diseased spots which fester and corrupt, where germs of every kind of disease collect - the places where our soldiers and sailors mostly spend their time. And the public-house is never by itself. Close to it - perhaps on either side of it - are houses of shame and evil. I would to God that the doctors in the naval and military hospitals could let their opinion of these places be known by the thinking people in England.

At any rate, I soon discovered that the Nonconformist ministers were only too anxious to move with me, with a view to drawing attention to these and other evils, which we considered to be a perpetual menace to the true health of our town. And then, to my greater joy, I found that Canon Jacob, and many of the Church clergy, too, were most anxious to join in the matter, and in a short time a Vigilance Committee had been appointed, which practically represented all that was best in every church and chapel, trade and profession, in the town of Portsmouth. Canon Jacob, who has since become Bishop of Newcastle, was elected chairman of that Committee, and I have never known anyone discharge duties - very difficult duties - with greater tact and earnestness.

On March 15th, 1894, the Town Council received a deputation from the Vigilance Committee upon the state of the streets in the town, and the Watch Committee, to whom the questions were referred, gave instructions to the Chief Constable, and the effect in a very short time was very manifest. The outward visible signs of the evil largely disappeared, and it was quite possible for people to walk through the streets without having their ears filled with the most disgusting language, and their sense of shame continually wounded. The lighting too of many streets, and especially of Southsea Common, by electricity, had a most desirable effect. But the real gain of the whole question was a deepening, in the minds of thoughtful men, of their duty in seeing that the authorities of the town did all that lay in their power to prevent temptation being forced on unwilling persons, and to make it possible for any lad or girl to go through any of the streets without being molested. When the town realises this duty, the authorities will soon see that that which is necessary is done.

On 18th August, 1894, the Society presented to the Licensing Justices an Open Letter, from which I have already quoted some statistics. This letter, at any rate, convinced the people of two facts: first, that the public-houses were altogether out of proportion to the population; secondly, that practically the monopoly of the drink traffic was held by a very few firms of brewers. When first I went to Portsmouth, and discovered how very undesirable many of the public-houses in my district were, I realised that it was utterly impossible that the brewers could know the character of the places in which their money was made, and I was particularly anxious that they should send their wives, or a lady of their acquaintance, dressed simply, to stay in their public-houses from 8.30 till the closing hour. I was told that this was an utterly preposterous demand. I cannot for the life of me see why it should be. The brewer makes his money, which his wife spends, out of the public-house. It is of vital importance that he should see, through the eyes of someone he can trust, how the money is made. If it is a place where he will not allow his wife to go, surely it is not a place where he wishes any other man's wife to go, or indeed any woman's husband, or indeed any other man or woman. And that is just the point I have never been able to understand about brewers. Many of them are most religious, excellent men, many of them even philanthropists, and doubtless these do see that all their public-houses are well-conducted. Some brewers say to me, "So long as the police do not interfere, it is no business of mine." But surely that is not a true basis on which to work. The publican is the servant of the brewer, very often the tied and bound servant, and the brewer has no more right to make a penny out of a house where there is any wrong going on, than he has to steal. I am perfectly sure that, if every brewer, putting aside for a moment his business manager and agent, would make either in his own person, or in the person of someone whom he really trusts and whom the publican does not know, an examination of his own houses, many of them would be shut up.

In Lent, 1894, I was asked to preach in London on the subject of sailors, and I expressed pretty freely my own views, saying that most naval towns, Portsmouth among them, were sinks of iniquity. I had

said the same thing over and over again in Portsmouth, and so I was
utterly astonished when I arrived at the railway station, on my
return, to discover the extraordinary storm my words had created.
Underlying all this righteous indignation there was a certain amount
of selfishness. Southsea, the favoured infant of the Corporation, for
whose sake Kingston and Landport are sometimes starved, was
endangered. If these words preached in London, and reported
throughout the kingdom in the public press, were believed, it might
hinder the influx of visitors, and so injure hotels, boarding-houses,
and shopkeepers. When a scare from want of proper drainage or
water has injured a health resort, is it wiser to try and hush the
matter up, and blame the man who has dragged the nuisance to light,
or to cure the nuisance, and render the town really healthy? That was
the question which the Mayor ought to have answered, though,
indeed, that part of it had never entered into my head. I only wanted
to make England at large realise the cruel injury which was done to
her noblest and best sons by the depravity which reigns in those very
spots where, for her sake, the truest and noblest of her children are
compelled to live. The Mayor's defence of the town was most
splendid. I venture to copy a few words from one of his speeches.

* * * * * *

"After this stigma has been thrown upon us, I have considered it
my duty, within the last twenty-four hours, to visit that part of the
town which has been spoken of so much - for there is no doubt what
part was meant in this gentleman's sermon. I started last night at
9.40, in company with an inspector of police, and I have in my hand
a report which I shall be pleased to hand to the rev. gentleman. I
visited 50 public-houses and beerhouses in the worst part of the
borough, between the hours of 9.40 and 11 p.m. At each house I took
the number of persons drinking, or sitting down, or talking, and in
the 50 houses there were 460 men and women. Where would you
send these people to? Are you going to let them walk about in the
streets? The upper ten can afford to belong to a club, and may not the
working man go and have his glass of beer and enjoy it? In the whole
of these 50 houses I may tell you - and tell you honestly, because I
have two witnesses to corroborate what I say - there was not one
drunken man on the premises, and during the time we were out we

saw in the streets only one man who was "jolly," and we cannot say
he was drunk. Surely with 10,000 sailors in port and nearly 6000
troops in garrison, I am not saying too much when I say we are proud
of our town. And I feel I must compliment the brewers and the
occupiers of public-houses and beerhouses of the town for the
admirable manner in which those houses are conducted. Do not let it
go forth that I just opened the doors and looked in. We went into the
bars, the taprooms, and the singing-rooms, and there was nothing
whatever that any man need be ashamed of seeing. I maintain that if
the rev. gentleman or anyone else would only take the trouble, as I
did last night, to go round to these houses and see the way in which
they are conducted, we should have no trouble in removing in a
moment the scandal and stigma which has been thrown on this
borough. You may leave the matter in the hands of your
representatives, and I feel sure that they will uphold the dignity of
the ancient borough of Portsmouth and look after your interests, and
that they will do all they can, as they have done before, to answer
those who talk to draw money to raise churches and other buildings.
We have to determine in our own minds whether this sermon, to
which I have referred, was preached in order to raise money to build
a church; if so, I would say that I should be sorry to go and pray in a
church built from money raised by stigmatising a town as this
clergyman has done."

I was threatened with a public indignation meeting in the Town
Hall. I only wish that Mr. Joseph and myself had had the chance of
addressing such a meeting. We wanted to ask the Mayor whether
there was any other town in England in which, between the hours of
9.40 p.m. and 11 p.m. - that is eighty minutes - fifty public-houses
could be entered, let alone thoroughly visited; whether he knew
anything of the character of the houses which he passed in going
from public to public; whether it could be desirable for the
inhabitants to have so many licensed premises so close together; and
whether he believed that there were fifty other publics anywhere in
England which, at that hour in the evening, were without people
whom he would call "jolly." Surely his defence was the very best proof
possible of my allegation. However, the public meeting never came

off; discretion was the better part of valour.

I believe myself that the row did the town a great deal of good, and I am thankful to think that when I left it two years after I received from all kinds and sorts of people the most appreciative letters, one of the very kindest being from one of the largest brewers. There is one splendid thing about English rows, that, though we hit as hard as ever we can, we do not seem to bear any malice. I hope everyone will believe that it was with the purest intention of trying to remedy evils, the removal of which will only make Portsmouth more glorious, a better home for our soldiers and sailors, a more attractive spot in which to make all patriotic Englishmen learn to value the magnificence of their own country, that I spoke every word that I ventured to say.

XI.
Our Battles Ecclesiastical.

IT has been easy to write of our battles with the brewers and brothel-keepers, for their attacks were in the open; but of our battles with our Bishops it is much more difficult to write, there being a dread in my own mind whether I have been able to judge perfectly fairly concerning their attitude towards us. And therefore I think it right to print in full the whole of the last correspondence between the Bishop of Winchester and myself, as nothing would distress me more than to put a wrong interpretation upon his action. Before I came there had been in the public press, and even at meetings, very violent attacks made upon Dr. Linklater. Portsmouth is a very Protestant town, and I had not been in it a week before I discovered that one must expect many attacks. Almost every week there were several very angry letters in the local press, and from time to time a big indignation meeting. The Protestant Hall had just been built, and it was evidently felt that it was a pity not to use it. But the letters and the meetings were about on an equality of common sense and charity, and I am quite sure we pursued the right method in never answering such attacks upon us. Sometimes the attack would be about ritual, sometimes about doctrine. I tried as far as I could in instructions in church to explain everything we did, but I do not suppose our opponents cared to come to our church, and therefore they were not benefited. I have often since then thanked God for this opposition, because it was the reason why we took such pains with our own people.

I felt, however, that upon some subjects, like Confession, very plain words must be spoken. Of course, amongst the boys and men in a parish like ours, it was the most needed of all church discipline, and it was just the one upon which the most horrid and untruthful things were being said. So I took heart of grace, and advertised throughout the town that on Sunday afternoon I would preach on the subject of Confession to men alone. I think I felt a little nervous, when I got into church and found it crammed from end to end, men even standing in the aisles, but I found that the vast majority, at any rate, were prepared to give me fair play, and they soon silenced those who had come merely to create a disturbance. I think what astonished them most was to hear that Confessions were heard in public, and that anybody who pleased could be in church at the time. I showed them exactly where the priest sat and where the penitent knelt, and I remember quite well saying, "If any of you, while coming from your work on Friday afternoon, look in, you will very likely see me hear a Confession." Accepting my advice, on the next Friday many people looked in at the door. I know that when they talked it all over in the Dockyard afterwards the verdict was arrived at, that, even if I was mistaken, I was straight and honest.

After a time, it was in 1887, we heard of a petition to the Bishop, signed at a large meeting, at which a gentleman from London had made a very violent attack on me, ending up with the magnificent peroration, "If we had a clergyman like Mr. Dolling in our neighbourhood, we would soon take him by the back of the neck, and kick him out of the parish." Before the meeting had time to applaud this most Christian sentiment, some lad, who had got into the gallery, shouted out, "He weighs fifteen stone, and you might find it difficult." The meeting collapsed in roars of laughter, but the petition was forwarded. I never thought for a moment that any reasonable person would have taken any notice of such proceedings, but, to my amazement, a few days afterwards I received a letter from Bishop Harold Browne, in which, beginning - "No doubt you are aware that there have been paragraphs and letters in various newspapers about your proceedings at S. Agatha's, and that there was an indignation meeting at the 'Protestant Hall,' with resolutions, etc., all of which have been sent to me with strong appeals. I do not think the persons appealing to me have any *locus standi*" - he desired that I would restrain my services to "the confessedly legal ritual of the Church of England," and also offered me the following considerations:

i. I am told that your own people generally, though attached to you, would prefer a less pronounced ritual.

ii. I believe with good reason that those clergy in Portsea who are doing great work in formerly neglected regions, feel that the scare produced by advanced ritual is seriously detrimental to them.

I wrote back that, if he ordered me, I was perfectly willing to obey the Prayer Book, and to have no other services, but that I felt my duty to my people made it incumbent upon me to impress the fact upon him that such change of services would mean a great diminution in the congregations, especially on the week-days, when the services complained of were used, and that I should like to know who had been his informant, as regards the wishes of my parish, and the opinion of my brethren in Portsmouth. His answer was, "I know that many of the clergy, by whom I certainly do not mean Mr. Young or Mr. Aldwell, regret your action, as calculated to throw suspicion upon all Church work. I do not wish to define legal ritual, but to suggest that you should be satisfied with what is purely Anglican, as sufficient for all purposes of devotion, and not liable to create suspicion, or to stir up strife. Stations of the cross, acolytes in crimson cassocks, incensing the Magnificat, and the like, certainly excite bitter animosity in an eminently Protestant town like Portsmouth. I have had no appeal from your own immediate district."

I know many people think that ritual rows have generally been the result of a clergyman endeavouring, to intrude his own methods upon an unwilling congregation, but I give these extracts from the Bishop's letters to show that at S. Agatha's that has never been the case. No complaint has ever come from one single parishioner. The complaints that have come have been made either by ignorant Protestants, or by my brethren the clergy.

However, at the end of 1889, the Bishop again wrote to us on the subject of ritual, and the following letter from the Bishop of Guildford, which, though it was marked "private," he has kindly allowed me to print, will show the five points to which the Bishop took exception.

"THE CLOSE, WINCHESTER,
"December 9, 1889."

MY DEAR MR. DOLLING,

"I am looking forward with much hopefulness to our interview with the Bishop on Thursday next. I did not go into any particulars in reply to your letter, in which you expressed your readiness to obey the Bishop if you were told by him to obey the P. Book, but that that would involve your reducing your services to a most dreary type. I am sure that on reflection you will have seen that the Bishop could never bring himself to make any recommendation which would bring down your services to such a low level as you suggest. But may there not be a *via media?* My object in writing to you, however, now (without the Bishop's cognisance, and, therefore, without knowing whether he would agree with me) is to ask you whether, at his request, you would be willing to give up using

"i. Incense at Celebrations and at the Magnificat.

ii. Service of Compline, in which, as far as I can gather, the choir practically absolve the priest.

iii. Extempore prayer.

iv. Vespers of the Blessed Sacrament in Cope.

v. Vespers for the Dead.

"If I could think that you would be ready to meet the Bishop with these concessions, it seems to me that you would still have your service with all its essential ritual and beauty, with only certain excrescences, as it seems to me, lopped off; and I am sure that you would find our Bishop most anxious to meet you in any way he could, and only too glad to be able to show his appreciation of your unwearied labours in our Master's cause. It seemed to me so sad that there should be any misunderstanding keeping you apart from our Bishop, that I have ventured thus to act as a sort of go-between, and earnestly to express my hope - nay, my prayer - that God may bring good out of our meeting on Thursday. I am sure you will be happier in your work, if even some things have to be given up, if you gain, on the other hand, your Bishop's approval of your work.

"Always I am,

"Your very faithful friend,
"GEORGE HENRY GUILDFORD.
"REV. R. DOLLING."

In a succeeding chapter you will read the reasons why I
introduced these services, and why I felt I could not possibly
surrender them. The objections to Compline and extempore prayer
seemed to me most extraordinary, but I am especially glad to insert
the letter, because it is a proof of the great kindness with which
Bishop Harold Browne and his Suffragan always treated us, and to
show that even though we differed, there was never anything but the
most cordial goodwill between us.

I think I have said that I was in the habit of preaching to men
alone on Sunday afternoons. Osborne, my fellow-priest, and I
thought that the time had come now for striving to get the ear of at
least some of the thousands of Dockyard-men who passed our church
on week-days, and so we asked the Guild of S. Matthew to send us
down a set of preachers for the six Sundays in the Lent of 1890. Mr.
Stewart Headlam was the first of these preachers. Osborne and I
listened to the sermon with very great attention, and we did not
discover in it anything different from the lectures which he and I had
been continually delivering in S. Agatha's. To our utter astonishment
we received almost immediately the letter from the Bishop which I
print.

"FARNHAM CASTLE, SURREY,
"*February 28, 1890.*
"MY DEAR MR. DOLLING,
"After what passed between us here some weeks ago, I was hardly
anticipating that I should have to remonstrate with you on a farther
and far more serious cause for difference between us.

"Without any intimation to me you invite a clergyman to teach in
your chapel, who has been inhibited by his own Bishop for teaching
on the very subject on which you advertise him as a preacher.
Anything more contrary to every law of the Church Catholic or the
Church of England it is difficult to imagine.

"If the report in the newspaper be correct, he, Mr, Stewart

Headlam, delivered a highly inflammatory political address, calculated to set class against class, and drawing down from an excited audience frequent expressions of applause, in a building devoted to Christian worship and called by you S. Agatha's Church.

"The teaching, according to *The Evening News*, was of this kind. Mr. Headlam represented our Lord's mission, not as intended to lead men to heaven, nor, apparently, to convert them to greater holiness, nor to reveal to them great spiritual truths, nor even to set up a great spiritual kingdom upon earth; but to establish a commonwealth in which there should be social equality and community of wealth (or poverty), from the good-will of all the members if possible, but, if not so, then from compulsion exercised by the many on the few.

"I have tried hard to see if the words can mean anything but this. I cannot possibly interpret them otherwise. The evil of such teaching appears to me incalculable. It is the substituting of a Political Christ for the loving Saviour of the world, a carnal kingdom for the great spiritual kingdom of the Church, earthly hopes and aspirations for divine and heavenly, and instead of love of the brethren springing from love of their Lord, a great probability, at least, of a system of plunder and terrorising such as prevailed in the French Revolution, and has been threatened of late by Nihilists and Communists. The theory that our Blessed Lord was a Social Reformer with a tinge of religious fanaticism is the favourite theory of political unbelievers. I do not mean to charge Mr. Headlam with holding this. But his teaching plays into the hands of such. I have always thought it to be the only theory which unbelievers can advance, with any appearance of plausibility, to account for the teaching and the success of Christ. The danger, therefore, of giving standing ground for such a theory is not easily exaggerated.

"I am not indifferent to varieties of ritual and the like; but tapers, and incense, and red-vested acolytes, nay! Romanism, Methodism, and any other varieties of Christian worship may be compatible with true faith in Christ and true love to Him and His. This so-called Christian Socialism, as exhibited in the report of Mr. Headlam's address, in the writings of Count Leo Tolstoi and others, appears to me to strike at the very root of all Christianity. I have, as you know, declined to interfere with your proceedings, lest I should mar your

Mission work. If you are to introduce teachers of such strange doctrines into a church or chapel, which you hold by virtue of my license, I must consider whether the good of our Mission is not more than neutralised by the evil of those whom you associate with you; and whether I can suffer it to go on under my authority. I am very sorry to write so strongly, but I dare not be indifferent.

"I am, dear Mr. Dolling,

"Very truly yours,

"G. H. WINTON."

In my answer I tried to point out to the Bishop, first, that Mr. Headlam had never been inhibited, and, secondly, that while I would, in deference to him, have the lectures delivered in the gymnasium instead of in the church, I must protest against the way in which he had spoken of the lecturers. Several other letters passed between us, but in the meantime Canon Jacob had written to the Headmaster of Winchester (I insert a letter he wrote to me), had withdrawn his subscription from the Mission, and had written to the Bishop to say what he had done.

"PORTSEA VICARAGE,

"March 3rd, 1890.

"DEAR MR. DOLLING,

"I have read with much pain, in the *Hampshire Post* and the *Hants Telegraph*, the report of Mr. Stewart Headlam's sermon at S. Agatha's. I sent a copy of the former paper on Friday to Dr. Fearon, and told him my extreme pain at finding my Old School Mission identified with such doctrines.

"I have gone on subscribing £1 1s. a year to your work through the Old Wykehamist Mission, in spite of much that I could not approve, but this has reached a limit which makes it necessary for me to reconsider the whole position. I do not wish to take any action inconsiderately, or without careful thought. It may be that you have explanations to offer. But I think it right to tell you at once that I am deeply pained to find how much you have added to our already sad

and unhappy divisions.
   "I am, faithfully yours,
   "EDGAR JACOB."

I also received from the Warden of Winchester College letters of
the strongest condemnation, letters, the first of which is signed
"Warden," in which he says Mr. Headlam is a Socialist in the bad
sense of the word; and of myself, that, with my ultra High Church
proclivities on the one hand, and Socialist teaching on the other, no
sober and loyal-minded citizens can be expected to support the
Mission, and that his connection with it must be severed, so long as I
remained the head of it.

I felt that Canon Jacob and the Warden must be taken in a large
measure to represent Wykehamical feeling, not, perhaps, just those
few who knew me and S. Agatha's well, but that large number who
supported the Mission, and that, therefore, there was no alternative
left me but to resign. So on Sunday morning I preached a sermon
defending the line I had taken, and at the same time telling the
people that I thought for peace it was better for me to leave. Never
can I forget the kindness of Dr. Fearon, other Winchester masters,
and old Wykehamists during the next week. Letters from all kinds
and sorts of people, whom we had never heard of, came to us, hoping
that we would not resign, and presently I received a letter from the
Warden, in which he told me that he had only written in his private
capacity, and that he did not represent either the school or anybody
else but himself. I felt very strongly, too, not only the kindness of
people outside, but the devotion of our people at home; and it
seemed to me a plain duty that, if Winchester wished me to remain, I
should do so. This duty was rendered all the more imperative by the
very great desire expressed by the Bishop himself that I should
remain.

As we have no legal status, the Mission not being a parish, a
change of Bishops is a matter of great importance, and I looked
forward with some anxiety to Bishop Thorold's coming. So it was
with much thanksgiving that I received this answer from him, soon
after his appointment, to a letter of mine about confirmation.

"BUTE HOUSE, CAMPDEN HILL, W.,
"16th January, 1891.

"DEAR MR. DOLLING,

"I am glad to hear from you, for I have heard much of you and your duty.

"Soon I hope to ask you here to dine and sleep, that we may have some talk about your difficult work, which has a charm and interest for me. We have eight such missions in South London, and I have fostered them as with a father's love.

"We will see about the Confirmation, but I prefer to do my work myself, if in my power.

"When you write again, perhaps you will be able to write all your letter yourself, 'a lot of time' for preparation is scarcely classical.

"May the blessing of the Holy Spirit rest upon you, and the sheep in the wilderness.

"Ever truly yours,

"A. W. ROFFEN."

Dr. Harold Browne had always refused to come to S. Agatha's, but he had allowed us to choose the Bishop who, from year to year, confirmed our people. But here was a Bishop who was not only coming himself, but who evidently was going to throw himself, heart and soul, into our work, and with the sufficient humour which just enables a man to slide over the difficulties of life. This goodness towards us, and endeavour to help us, never once ceased during the four years in which he ruled our diocese. My heart is often sorry for hard words I may have said about him.

In a week or two he asked me to stay with him in London, and we talked for many hours. He drew out from me every detail of our work, approving or disapproving, but ever ready to hear reasons, telling me quite plainly that there was much he liked, much he disliked. Especially was he interested in our schools - he thought we had been very brave in gaining them - in our house, in which he hoped soon to stay; and, above all, in our temporary church, and the manner of our memorials, the lists of soldiers, sailors, emigrants, the confirmed, and the blessed dead; and this led to explaining to him how we used the Holy Communion as our best and most prevailing intercession. He had been delighted when I told him that at our prayer meetings these names were read out, but I am quite sure that at first, at any rate, he was shocked at people coming to the celebrations for intercession and not for communion. I explained to him how impossible it was for our people to communicate frequently, the stress of their business and their ignorance making preparation very difficult; and, I think, from words he let fall, that he considered we were in some sense lowering the dignity of the Blessed Sacrament by permitting it to be used for any other purpose but communion, though he told me himself how often his best intercessions were made when he was receiving communion. This did not apply to intercessions for the dead. He evidently disbelieved in any such being beneficial to them, or helpful to the persons making them; but we prayed long in his study, after family prayers were over, and I felt that I had gained one who, whatever our differences were, would act towards me as a real father. The next morning, walking round and round his beautiful garden - a wonderful oasis in the overcrowded desert of Kensington, alas! now pulled down and turned into flats; I could almost cry as I look at it, when I pass Campden Hill each Sunday morning this Lent - he talked over the matter again and again, specially desirous that I should discontinue the Mass for the Dead, and that I should never have a celebration without communicants. I told him - I hope with all dutifulness - that these two requests were impossible; the first because I considered I was exercising one of the greatest privileges of my priesthood, and because this special office for the dead had been a wonderful help to many of our poor people - an act of real reparation for stumbling-blocks they had put in the way of companions now beyond their reach by any other method, and also because the remembrance of the dead kindles and draws out, even in the most brutish, an understanding of the supernatural, which becomes a realisation of hope otherwise impossible; the second because it would be impossible for the clergy and workers to bear the burden of toil and responsibility that rested upon us every hour of the day, if it were not for the help of those daily morning-celebrations, and that the only method by which that rubric as to communicants, could be obeyed, would be by compelling my workers to take turns - three on Monday, three on Tuesday, &c. - however much indisposed they might feel at the moment to make their communions. He said at once that this would be a most hateful method, and I left him knowing that we were going to continue these two things of which he disapproved; but he did not forbid them, and his last words showed me that he was fully prepared to trust us. I think what pleased him most was what he called our straightforwardness and honesty; and I thank God that neither then nor since have I ever hid anything from him.

His stay with us, when he came to confirm, very considerably deepened our mutual affection. The confirmation was to be at eight p.m. The people began to come into church at seven, according to their custom. I always delighted in this hour before the confirmation as giving an opportunity by extempore prayers, by heads for intercession, and by singing hymns, of getting the friends of the candidates into a proper frame of mind. The candidates knew exactly their places, for they had sat in them at the three previous Sunday nights' Mission services. They knew exactly, too, in what order they were to go up to the Bishop. Many a confirmation - indeed, many a first communion too - has lost all its grace from want of preparation, not of the heart, but of the mode of reception. The Bishop had been quite hurt when he found that only a curate had been sent to meet him; but I think when he opened the west door of S. Agatha's, and saw the church quite full, people in the aisles as well as in the seats, kneeling in humble prayer between each verse of "When I survey the wondrous cross," he forgave me for not meeting him. In the vestry I said to him, "The service, of course, is yours. You will make whatever arrangement you like about acolytes, &c." He asked those in red cassocks to take them off, and when I told him that a crucifix was always carried in the procession, he asked that it might be put away; but when I told him that there was one on the high altar, he said, "Oh, I shall not see that one!" No words of mine can fittingly express his tenderness towards those he confirmed. More than half of them were grown men and women, many of them, whose former lives could hardly be told about, drawn from the lowest slums by the attractive power of the Cross, with a real and true belief in the grace which they were about to receive at his hands, with a humility and yet perfect trust which the soul, conscious of its own weakness and of

Christ's power to save, alone experiences.

Meanwhile in our own house small difficulties had arisen. The Bishop, whose digestion even at that time was greatly impaired, had kindly sent us on a little sheet of paper his menu, headed, "What I desire to eat," a morsel of fish, a mutton chop, a rice pudding. But he had not told us that he was going to bring a servant, and would use some particular kind of sheets. When I got in I heard that Mary was disturbed, and the disturbance of Mary was no small matter in our household, because, finding the servant putting on these sheets, her honour was grievously wounded, she deeming the Bishop thought that the beds in our house were dirty. However, things righted themselves. Our rule of common food had to be broken through, as the servant objected to meal with the Bishop, and fed somewhere by himself. One could see how utterly overtired Bishop Thorold was, but he put that altogether on one side, and evinced the kindest interest in all our inmates, until at last, when he could speak not another word, he went off to bed; and yet I never shall forget how fatigue was conquered in the long, earnest, loving intercession he offered to Almighty God for me and mine.

The next morning he examined the old church very attentively, remarked upon what he considered the ugliness of our little altar, on which there were painted in panels a priest in black vestments saying Mass for the Dead; and a soul being carried by angels into paradise; again told us he disapproved altogether of prayers for the dead, and yet more of Masses, but never said one word to forbid them, and then drove off to the garrison church, where he was going to confirm. I had looked forward with considerable dread to his coming. I knew he wanted to like us, but I was terribly afraid of the ordeal. But after the visit I believed that through his episcopate there would be nothing but peace between us. However, the enemy was not going to give us peace, and in November, 1892, we noticed a gentleman attending the children's Mass armed with a pair of opera-glasses. I urged him to go into the front pew, where he would not have to use them, thereby disturbing the congregation. Very shortly afterwards I received from the Bishop a long document sent to him by the Protestant Alliance, and asking me particulars about the service, and to send him the children's Mass book. On December 16th I received the following letter from him.

"FARNHAM CASTLE, SURREY,
"December 16, 1892.

"DEAR MR. DOLLING,

"With respect to the Sunday School Book now in use at S. Agatha's Mission Chapel, I do not feel that this is a moment when I can equitably press upon you to withdraw it from use.

"My opinion, however, as to the grave inconsistency of its contents with our Anglican standards remains unchanged, and though it may be a matter of indifference to you, it is a matter of real concern to me that the influence and development of a mission conducted with such zeal and self-denial should be in any way prejudiced in the eyes of those whose prayers and sympathy ought not to go for nothing in your eyes, by the use of a manual not vital to your ministrations, and but scantily adopted in the Church.

"It is my hope and desire that you will consider the wisdom and duty of quietly discontinuing it, when you can do so without loss of self-respect, or feeling of giving way to ignorant clamour; and I shall hope to hear from you before Trinity Sunday that you have found yourself able to comply with this advice."

Very truly yours,

"A. WINTON."

I answered back at once, that I was quite ready to withdraw the book, and to substitute another in its place, but that for my own sake I should like to prove to him that there was no expression in it which might not be discovered in the writings of the great Anglican divines, and he wrote that he would be very glad to receive such a catena. Dear Osborne at once set to work on a library of the Anglo-Catholic Fathers, which we bought for the purpose, and submitted a defence to the Bishop. Indeed the Bishop was kind enough to ask both of us to go to Farnham. I think he was rather astonished when we arrived with a large trunk full of books, but he was very patient while Osborne, who is a theologian, which I am not, expounded out of Bramhall, Andrewes, and others, that there has been a continual witness, oftentimes on the part of the most learned prelates and authorities in the Church of England, to the right to believe and to teach within its fold the doctrine of pleading the Blessed Sacrament for the living and the dead, as was taught in the little book.

This very characteristic letter left only one course possible to us, the writing of a new book, which we did at once.

"FARNHAM CASTLE, SURREY,
"January 21, 1893.

"DEAR MR. DOLLING,

"I have now read, and with much interest, the extracts from the writings of eminent Anglican divines on Eucharistic doctrine, which you have collected with so much industry and laudable anxiety to justify your own position.

"While I cannot admit - and in this you will doubtless concur with me - that the i*pse dixit* of any individual, eminent and learned though he be, can accurately be quoted as the mind of the Church at large, I have no wish to demur to the authorities you quote as undeserving of great reverence and consideration. It is also particularly agreeable to me, though I have never expressed any doubt on the subject, to be assured that your great desire is to be loyal to Anglican standards and teaching, and that you have not knowingly transgressed them in this instance.

"You will remember that on your own teaching I pronounced no opinion whatever. It was the book used at S. Agatha's that seemed to deserve, and I still think deserves, my grave remonstrance.

"After thinking it well over, I am clear that I should prefer the withdrawal of the book, and your substituting for it one of your own compiling. You will not be unwilling to introduce into such a book, nor ashamed of so doing, more of the exact language of our Prayer Book and of our Lord Himself. While it would be inconsistent for me to sanction a book which from your own point of view might in some of its statements widely diverge from that I hold to be sound teaching, I could at least protect you in the use of it. The last thing in the world I intend or desire is to limit in the very least degree the liberty of the clergy to hold and teach what may equitably be held to be supported and countenanced by our standards. You know me well enough to trust me when I say that I value your work, recognise your

sacrifices, cherish your friendship, and will gladly, so far as I can, strengthen your hands.
"Your friend and father in God,
"A. WINTON."

But in the meanwhile, to his astonishment as well as ours, a letter not intended for publication, which he had written to the Secretary of the Protestant Alliance, appeared in the papers:

"FARNHAM CASTLE, SURREY.
"Sir,
"Since acknowledging your memorial, I have procured and examined the S. Agatha's Sunday School Book, and have also referred it to one of my examining chaplains, in whose learning and judgment I have great confidence. While I do not consider that all the passages in it on which you have animadverted can he accurately pronounced to be as distinctly Roman in doctrine as you have not unreasonably conceived them to be, the general substance of the book is, in my opinion, quite irreconcilable with the Eucharistic teaching of the Church of England; nay, I have no hesitation in saying that I consider the general atmosphere and phraseology of the volume to be even more objectionable and dangerous, than any of the precise expressions which have caused you such intelligible offence.
"It is right, however, that I should here explain that, if I am correctly informed, the officiating clergyman, when this book is used, himself says nothing except what is in the Common Prayer Book.
"At the present moment I am in correspondence with Mr. Dolling on the subject; but I wish at once to observe that his work at S. Agatha's, though disfigured by errors and eccentricities, which, in common with not a few of his truest friends, I sincerely deprecate, is of a kind which very few other men are capable of accomplishing, and reaches a class of society too frequently left to itself out of sheer helplessness and despair.
"I have twice confirmed in S. Agatha's Chapel, and have stayed a night under Mr. Dolling's roof, and have given myself ample opportunity for observing and gauging the nature of his work, and the measure of his personal influence in the neighbourhood where he

resides. In my opinion, the substantial good he is enabled to effect by his self-denying and Christian activities far outweighs by its usefulness any distress that may be caused to those who are gravely alarmed by doctrines and practices which they consider to be quite inconsistent with the standards of the Reformed Church.

"With this view I hope to be able to continue to him my support and countenance, in the belief that he will again be ready, as he has already shown himself to be ready, to accept my fatherly direction, when responsibly and kindly offered. Hereby he will move out of the way of his undisputed usefulness causes of offence which alienate outside sympathy and disappoint sincere well-wishers on the spot, and will also, if at the sacrifice of some cherished convictions, strengthen his own cause, and help the work he loves.

"I am, your faithful servant,

"A. WINTON."

At first it seemed that, in justice to ourselves, it would be necessary to print the whole of our correspondence with the Bishop, and our defence of the little book. But, after thinking the matter over, it seemed best to leave things as they were. After all, it was no business of the public, and the question would only have opened up a controversy which would have done more harm than good. But the Bishop, with extraordinary generosity, sent me a letter, which he allowed me, if I thought it would serve a good purpose, to print:

"FARNHAM CASTLE, SURREY,
"February 6, 1893.
"DEAR MR DOLLING,

"It was as disappointing to me as it must have been distressing to you, that my reply to the complaint of the Secretary to the Protestant Alliance, in which I do not find a syllable about his intention to publish it, should have been sent to the papers without my knowledge or sanction. But for our friendship all hopes of arrangement might have been wrecked.

"You have intimated your willingness to withdraw the book of which complaint has been made, and I think reasonably, and to prepare another to be used in its place. I trust that the new one will be less liable to misconstruction than the one you are using now. While I have neither the desire nor the right to arrogate to myself an infallible interpretation of the Church's standards, it is my plain duty to counsel, and even admonish, where it is made plain to me that there is a divergence from them. If this is not a Bishop's duty, one of the most solemn of his consecration vows becomes a hollow verbiage. I have no sort of intention of withdrawing from you the countenance and support which hitherto I have readily given to your work at S. Agatha's. To be consciously unjust to you is, I assure you, an impossibility for me. But justice to you implies some sort of justice to myself. You have never expected nor asked me to say that with all your methods and teaching I can profess sympathy. It is but straightforward for me to add that it is your self-denying life, with the manly, generous activities behind it which God is so manifestly blessing, that makes me more than ready to condone what I and others would with satisfaction find to be eliminated from your public services; and, in renewing an expression of my good-will and personal affection, I desire not to be thought to be acting inconsistently with the principles and aspirations of a ministry of 44 years.

"Sincerely yours,

"A. WINTON."

Nothing could exceed his kindness to us ever afterwards, and as his eye ever had a twinkle in it, so his kindness had ever a delightful playfulness. This letter of November 30th, 1893, will show how ready he was to meet our wishes at personal inconvenience to himself.

"THE DEANERY, WINCHESTER

"MY DEAR SIR,"

"In reply to your letter of the 27th instant, the Bishop of Winchester desires me to say that he has never yet fixed a day that suited you, and never expects to be so fortunate. But, of course, your confirmation shall be put off".

Faithfully yours,

"G. E. HITCHCOCK, CHAPLAIN."

This of March 28, 1894, was in answer to a request of mine for a general licence in his diocese, as I had none, and, as I had been elected to the Conference, it was supposed I might be objected to on those grounds.

"FARNHAM CASTLE, SURREY."

MY DEAR MR. DOLLING,

"A free lance will be wise to keep his freedom. With all good-will. "Yours, A. WINTON."

And this, of May 11, 1894, in explanation of a mistake he had made about Mr. Dowglass, whom I had asked him to license as our curate.

"FARNHAM CASTLE, SURREY."

MY DEAR MR. DOLLING,

"I receive your rebuke with becoming meekness. But if you had so many things of all sorts in your head as I have, and were continually on the drive, away from all books of reference, you would be merciful to me for not always recognising the identity of curates with not uncommon names.

"Mr. Dowglass has been excellently reported to me, and I am only too glad to have him in the diocese, and, of course, I will license him when his papers are ready, and sent in. With much contrition,

"I am, always faithfully yours,

"A. WINTON."

I might just add one proof of his real liberality. On the death of my friend and neighbour, Mr. Shute, who had created, with wonderful energy and untiring zeal, S. Michael's, the church next to ours, the Bishop offered the incumbency to my fellow-priest Osborne, who had so ably defended the little book which the Bishop had condemned.

He took, too, a continual interest in the building of our new church. He saw all the plans, and himself suggested that it would not need a new licence, so that all formality and red tape might be prevented. Above all he urged us to move in all our memorials, and to make the church as homely as we possibly could for our poor. A passion for the poor consumed his heart, and he seemed to have kept them and the outcast always in his mind, often asking me about someone whose story I had told him perhaps a year before, and not only treating me in his own house with the greatest tenderness and affection, but on public occasions like the Diocesan Conference, when I felt it my duty to say things about the Establishment and Social Questions, which few of my brethren agreed with, he always gained for me a patient hearing, and often said kindly things afterwards. Alas! if he had lived a little longer, I should have been still at S. Agatha's; and yet who could wish him to live, when every hour was but an agony, and only an intense sense of duty enabled him bravely to bear the burden of his flesh, which he was so willing to surrender at any moment into his loving Master's hands.

I am only sorry that my own angry passions and bitter way of looking at questions have, from time to time, moved me to say and write unkind and unworthy things about him. But from the first day I ever saw him I was conscious of a real love and affection, which deepened, until God took him, and which will ever remain in my mind as a special grace and gift of God, granted to me through four of the most difficult years of my life.

I had often talked with Bishop Thorold of a fitting time for me to leave Portsmouth, and he had agreed with me that, as soon as the people were accustomed to the new church, I might resign. We had hoped that the church might be opened on the first Sunday in October. It was the anniversary of my taking full charge of the Mission, and the progress of the parish had been marked each year by the dedication to the glory of God and the use of our people, of some special piece of parish machinery. I was greatly in need of rest, for my work, with its threefold responsibility at Landport, Winchester, and begging, was beginning to tell upon me, and for the last four years I had not had one single day's holiday. If the church were opened on the first Sunday in October, I thought it would be quite permissible for me to leave the following Easter, and I had told Dr. Fearon of this intention. When I announced this to our own people, they at once began to make every effort to induce me to alter my determination.

But in the meantime two circumstances had happened which disarranged all our plans. First, Bishop Thorold died; and secondly, we discovered the church could not be opened till quite the end of October. It had been my boast that the whole fabric of the church was completed by Portsmouth men, and I can never speak too highly of the punctuality and excellence of their work. The builders, Messrs. Light and Son - Portsmouth is mourning now the head of the firm, one of the most useful, honoured, and respected of its citizens - Townsend, the foreman, indeed all down to the men who mixed the mortar, and the boys who ran the messages, had striven to make the church the enormous success that it is. But we had employed a London firm to do the wood flooring and the marble work. Their workmen were Italians; and Light's men, all Trade Unionists, almost refused to work with them, because they said that they did not work for a proper rate of wages. However, the arrangement had been made, and so, though the foreman told me he was sure I would suffer for employing them, the work had to go on. They had a row amongst themselves their first Saturday, and one got stabbed in the hand, but, be the cause what it was, we found that the opening of the church must be delayed a month. On September 28th I wrote to Bishop Davidson, telling him that the church would be opened on October 27th, and saying that Dr. Thorold had thought that no new licence would be needed, as the old and the new church were practically joined together by the vestry. I heard from him on October 4th, saying that though he himself thought that it would be better that a new licence should be given to the new building, yet Bishop Thorold's opinion would justify us going forward with our arrangements, and that he would let us know later on. On October 17th we heard from him that he had considered the question of the new licence, and it seemed clear to him that it ought to be granted, and that the Rural Dean would visit us for the purpose of inspecting the building.

In the meantime a dear friend had told us that the Bishop was hurt at not being asked to take part in the opening services. The friend, I afterwards discovered, was perfectly mistaken in his judgment; but acting on that information, I wrote to the Bishop to explain why I had not asked him to be present at the opening, and I thought the best way to show him that no disrespect was intended was by telling him that I had not intended asking Bishop Thorold, because I knew that our manner of service would pain him very deeply.

On October 24th, I received a long letter from the Bishop, the purport of which was that he could not grant the licence, until a question so important as the third altar had been submitted to the proper authorities, or the altar itself had been removed, but saying that he would be glad to see me the next morning. And so on October 25th, I spent the morning at Farnham.

Nothing could exceed the Bishop's kindness and straightforwardness during that interview. He is a man of most delightful manners. A theologian at Oxford said of him, soon after his appointment to the Deanery of Windsor: "He is a Nuncio already," though he slily added, "but not from Peter." But I felt a good deal more than the mere charm of his manner. He was evidently conscious that we were both in a very difficult position. He seemed most desirous to do his duty towards me and my people, and deeply felt the responsibility that was resting on him. At the very outset of our conversation he said, "This is no red-tape question of three altars, but of the services said at those altars." When I proposed to him that we should continue in the old church until his judgment was pronounced, he seemed to feel that it would be a mistake to upset the existing arrangements, and that it would be better to screen off the third altar for the present and proceed with the opening. I gave in to his desire at once, though I had brought with me fifty-two telegrams ready for despatch should the opening be delayed. When I got home, those who worked with me were very distressed that I had not put off the opening, and I feel now that they were certainly right, and that much pain and a certain amount of scandal to the Church might have been saved if I had pursued this course.

So we opened the new church on October 27th. Dr. Fearon had arranged for the masters and men at Winchester to come down on the Monday after the opening, and I had asked the Bishop of Southwell, the founder of the Mission, to come and preach to them. He not only consented to do this, but offered to preach the first sermon in the new church on the Sunday morning at 11 o'clock. When he came down on the night before, he kindly sent word to say

that he would celebrate at 8 o'clock the next morning. There were
more than four hundred communicants at the four early services,
and at 11 we started to take possession of the new church. I, who
remembered the hooting and stoning of ten years ago, could hardly
believe it was the same place. Mr. Dyer-Edwardes, a great benefactor
to the Mission, had lent us a magnificent silver crucifix to be carried
in front of the procession, but everything else in the procession
belonged to the Mission. Dear Barratt, the truest friend a priest has
ever had, with the incense, and then our little choir lads, and our
choirmen, such loyal and earnest supporters of the Mission; then the
acolytes in red, most of whom had been with me ever since they were
little children, directed by Pennell, our ceremoniarius, then the
Bishop in his convocation robes, who, not desiring to pontificate,
walked before the unworthy priest who was to sing the first Mass in
the new S. Agatha's. Directly behind me, leading the congregation,
Mr. White and Mr. Claxon, who have acted as churchwardens during
the ten years, and then an innumerable number of parishioners and
old friends, who had come home for the day. There was, I think,
through the whole of that crowd, blocking up all the streets and
making it difficult for us to pass through them, but one attitude of
respect, I might even say of affection, and a realising, too, that a great
act of worship was being offered to that God, Who is our common
Father. If, when the procession entered the building, there was a
little unseemly rush, that was not to be wondered at. Even at S.
Peter's, in the presence of the Pope, English people do not always
behave reverently and well. But long before I had gained the altar
there was a hush of reverent devotion, and the wonderful beauty of
the church made itself, for the first time, manifest, its dignity and
simplicity, its fittingness for magnificent worship, and, above all, its
excellent acoustic properties - a proud moment, indeed, for Mr. Ball,
the architect, and if it had not been for the shadow which the
covering of the third altar threw over my troubled heart, a proud
moment for me.

Many letters, which will be found in an appendix, passed between
the Bishop and myself. On November 15th, at his kind invitation, I
spent a long morning at Farnham. I was suffering from a bad attack
of influenza at the time. The Bishop's position and mine were

naturally very difficult, for he had to discover matter for judgment out of the mouth of the accused. I am quite conscious of not being a theologian, and I answered as plainly and as simply as I could all his questions, and I am since aware that I used an expression, which he afterwards quoted in his judgment, which may be very liable to misconstruction. My intercourse with Dr. Thorold had been so very different. There had been perfect freedom in all conversations between us, nay more, I had often volunteered information which he had not asked for. A hundred times the memory of him flashed across my mind, and his many words of prayer came back again and again to my remembrance. I was sitting in the same study, but now I was accused, and I was conscious that my own and my people's happiness, nay, perhaps the safety of weak, timid souls, was hanging in the balance. I pray that none of my readers may ever have such an hour and a half as I passed at Farnham.

Meanwhile, until the Bishop's judgment was pronounced, only one duty lay before me - to go on as if nothing had occurred. My mind, however, since the opening of the church, had altered upon one point.

If the Bishop permitted it, I should be forced to remain much longer than Easter. I was told of a petition of over 5000 people, signed by all classes, and by people of all shades of opinion, wanting me to stay in Portsmouth. I discovered that the debt upon the church would be much greater than I had anticipated, so many things having to be added at the end. But, above all, I felt that it would take a considerable time to make new S. Agatha's really the home of the people. I knew, of course, that other priests could work much more consistently and successfully than I had done. That I never doubted for a moment. But I knew, too, that I was the only one who had ten years of experience teaching me how to deal with these particular people. On December 7th the Bishop's judgment came, and it left me, I conceived, no alternative but to resign, which I did the next day. I believed directly I read it that the judgment forbade us to say our Mass for the Dead, or to have Celebrations without Communicants. The surrender of these two points I felt it impossible to make. An error has largely arisen that I left because I could not have a third altar in my church, but this is quite incorrect. The Bishop, at the very commencement, said it was not a red-tape question of a third altar, but a question of the services said at that altar, and I myself, and my communicants, and a magistrate in the town, who thought that I had not been explicit in making it, made the offer that the altar should be moved, but the services maintained. I am condemned also, by many, for having been disobedient to the Bishop. Indeed, I think this was the reason why the Bishop of Durham prevented me preaching a Mission in his diocese. But I am sure that the Bishop of Winchester would be the first to say that this was not the case. In one sense, if I had wished to stay, it would have been very difficult to put me out. For I have created almost everything that exists at S. Agatha's, and I am either joint or sole trustee for all the property; and I am, even now, responsible for £3000 incurred either on the church or on property which has been recently acquired for the Mission purposes. I say this in no spirit of boasting, but only to set myself right with the public. If I were to express my private opinion, I should say it would have been much wiser for a Bishop just entering on his diocese to have let S. Agatha's, at any rate for a year or two, be ruled by the decision of his predecessor; but Bishop Davidson had every right to take a different view of the case, and, doubtless, he only put into action what is the mature judgment of many English Churchmen. One of the most learned and devoted of the High Church school has said that it is for the good of the body that excrescences should be cut off. I am an excrescence, ergo, when an opportunity arises, it is wise to lop me off. But, if mine is intended as an object-lesson, I fear it will hardly be so accepted by the other excrescences. They are all well sheltered by their freeholds, and few bishops to-day would like to undertake the odium of a ritual prosecution, far less the expense it entails. After all, too, the excrescence is not so unlike the healthy limb. It differs more in expression than in fact. By my resignation the Bishop gains two points. First, though my successor will, every Friday, say Mass for the Dead, he will only use outwardly the words of the Book of Common Prayer. Secondly, he has asked the communicants to arrange amongst themselves that there shall be three communicants at both the 10 and 11 o'clock Masses on Sundays. And this being so, he will say the part of the service relating to communicants. But he requests that they will come fasting, and

THE THIRD ALTAR

give him notice beforehand. His desire to obey the Prayer Book has, I think, landed him rather on the horns of a dilemma. If no one gives him notice, will he have the Celebration, using the Exhortation, Confession, and Absolution, knowing that no communicants will be present? Or, will he give up the 10 and 11 o'clock Celebrations? The same difficulty will apply to the week-day Masses. We condemn as a fundamental error the idea that men were created for the sake of the Sacraments. We believe that the Sacraments were created for the sake of men. But it seems that, by this new theory, men were created for the sake of the rubrics of the Book of Common Prayer. I make no complaint whatsoever. I have no right to make a complaint. And if, on the one hand, my conscience would have allowed me to say, for instance, this week the service for the second Sunday after Lent, in black vestments, or to have used a collect from the Visitation of the Sick, or from the Burial of the Dead, either saying them in a sense not intended by the Book of Common Prayer, or interpolating words of my own, and secretly to say the rest of the Office for the Dead; and, on the other, to invite people to make the most solemn of all our public confessions, and to pronounce Absolution over them, when I knew that not one of them was going to receive that Communion, which necessitated such a confession and warranted such an absolution, I should be still at S. Agatha's. There is one solemn question which I should like to ask those who lop us off. Do they wish that we should go into lay communion, and our work, as priests, be lost to the Church of England? Or do they want us to exercise our priesthood in another Communion? Before the old diocesans gaily commence their course of lopping, or a new diocesan, refusing to walk in the safer paths of his predecessors, proceeds to lop, I pray them pause and consider.

XII.
Our Money-Grubbing.

YOU so often hear it said now, "Only a rich man can afford to take that living, "I doubt if there could be any more dangerous idea about the position of the parish priest. Once let the parishioners, and the Church at large, imagine that the Vicar is going to pay everything out of his own pocket, and you destroy that most needed of all Christian duties - systematic giving. The false idea, so largely believed - that the clergy are all State-paid, and, therefore, well paid - is one of the reasons why, in so many places, members of the Church of England are utterly wanting in the duty of almsgiving. When Dr. Fearon chose me, he chose the poorest man in England. As I have told you, I had to pawn my watch on my first visit to the Bishop, and I believe that this is the very reason why God has so wonderfully blessed us with money. If we lived in mediaeval times, people might almost believe of the Mission the old legends of the miraculous multiplication of food and money, for there have been many occasions when we were literally without a penny; but those were the very times when money came to us the most strangely. And why should we doubt that miracles are wrought to-day? Though I could nearly always make a shrewd guess as to where the money came from, even if it came anonymously, still I know it came in answer to those two powers by which all miracles have been wrought - faith and prayer; not my own, indeed, for that often failed, but those of my helpers and my own people. I think the Bishop of Winchester must have felt something like this when he kindly came and saw round the Mission the week before we left. I could not, of course, show to him our real treasures - men and women, clothed, and in their right mind, sitting at the Saviour's feet, a few years back lost to all sense of shame and decency. I could not show him our Communicants' Society: it would have been putting too great a strain upon my people's patience. But I could show him the outward signs of our success - the changed streets, and the unmurmuring attitude of those who at once saw that he was the Bishop. Many years before I had helped to save his predecessor, when he was Bishop of Rochester, from being stoned in Lorimer Square; but I had no fear that even one rude word would be spoken to him. This, at any rate, was a discipline that our people had learned. I was able to show him, too, our wonderful gymnasium, the parsonage, the day-schools, the almshouses, the Mission-house, old S. Agatha's, and new S. Agatha's, nearly all of which had been built by my begging. I wonder if any thought passed through his mind that he was actually, at that moment, killing the goose that had laid the golden eggs - truly a goose, for was it wise to lay out ten years of one's life in effecting all this; indeed, to entail upon one's self future years of begging, without any assurance more than the implied consent of the Bishop for the time being that I should be permitted to finish it? But, surely, it is only the faithless who would think it was foolish. For to labour, and to know that others will enter into your labour, is but a necessary consequence of being the servant of a Church whose work is one and continuous, whomsoever it is done by; and our part is only to be as grateful as our niggardly natures allow us, because we have been permitted to share, ever so little, in the glorious work by which, to-day, the Church of England is restoring to herself her lapsed children. Whether it is prudent of rulers to kill the goose, is a different question; they know their own business best, and, at any rate, one admires those who have the courage to act upon their convictions. They, too, who see the poor at second-hand - that is, through the appeals which come to them - can hardly be expected to realise the awful burden and difficulty of begging. I calculate that I have devoted one day out of every week that I spent at Portsmouth to this work alone.

You will notice in the accounts, which I hope you will read, a very large item for postage and for travelling. This represents my begging machinery. Every quarter I sent out to every subscriber, and to-every man at Winchester, an account of the quarter's work. Few duties were more irksome than the writing of these reports. One was bound to tell the truth, and to tell it so as to interest. The days of writing these reports will be remembered by every inmate of our house. I have often heard new inmates told by old ones, "I would not ask him anything. He is in a raging temper to-day." At meals we all sat perfectly silent; even George Kerr, drinking his cod-liver oil between meat and pudding, or the antics and blandishments of the latest Buddha, could not make us smile. And if Mary heard a piano-organ coming anywhere near, she would run out with twopence to bribe them to go away. Everyone knew I was writing the report; everyone knew how much depended upon its success. I expect lots of the subscribers never read them; I am sure the majority of Winchester men did not. But, still, I believe they were the great means of keeping alive the knowledge of the Mission, and interest in it.

Then the begging by word of mouth. How extraordinarily kind people have been to us in this respect. I have got offertories in no less than eighty-one churches, and have spoken in drawing-rooms and public halls; I have been sandwiched into classical concerts and comic concerts; I have lectured in boys' schools and girls' schools, and have collected in this way £3137, and yet this sum does not all represent the actual amount received, for many a cheque came afterwards. I remember once preaching at a little church at Nice, and being very much annoyed with the clergyman for asking me, as there were only about ten people present; and yet there I discovered J. Dyer-Edwardes, who has been one of our greatest helpers, not only giving us money but supplying most delightful holidays for the clergy in his beautiful home in Gloucestershire. People at the meetings have always been so kind, but they generally remarked, "Oh, it evidently gives you no trouble to speak, you require no preparation." They little knew the sleepless nights which evolved perhaps one single joke, and the tremendous difficulty of speaking time after time on the same subject without getting exaggerated or inaccurate. This living in the train, too, is terribly distressing, especially if you always want to get home at night, and I never felt that I slept at ease away from home. A house like ours was a responsibility, even greater than getting the money to keep it going. In Lent preaching seven or eight courses in London besides all my sermons at home, I have come home two or three times a week by the midnight train, so much so that at last I found it cheaper to have a season ticket. Yet even this was a reproach, for people seeing me travel second class thought I was proud and extravagant; as was also a fur coat, which one of my sisters gave me, as I suffer greatly from the cold when travelling at night, for I heard a lady, who passed me when coming out of a vestry, say, "If I had known he had a coat like that, I should not have put five shillings in the collection." Then think of the moral deterioration of oneself. You look at everyone from the point of view, *What shall I get out of him?* Sneaking in at the vestry door you look round the corner to see if there are any carriages. And yet one does not grudge all this, for it means the larger part of £50,000 collected for the Church of England during ten years.

Of course in all this collecting Winchester has been our chief contributor. The men and masters were responsible for £150 of my salary. There is an offertory three times a year in chapel. The balance goes to a Central Wykehamist Fund, which is managed by a committee of members elected by present Wykehamists, with the Headmaster as chairman. This committee has sent me £11,292. But this does not represent at all what I have received from Wykehamists, past and present. Looking over the names of subscribers I should say I have received £15,000 more. I cannot be grateful enough for this money. Much of it has come from those, whom I know gave with difficulty. Much of it came from those who did not agree, some with my social, some with my religious, some with any of my opinions. But they gave it because they believed that a good work was being done in Landport, which reacted even upon the school itself.

A great deal of it has come, far more than one would believe, from the people of S. Agatha's. Gold is an unknown quantity almost in S. Agatha's offertories. When White and Claxon, who always counted the money, discovered a five-shilling piece, they nearly had a fit. And yet mostly in coppers, threepences, sixpences, and a few shillings, we averaged over £4 on general Sundays, with a considerable addition on any special day. Four years ago we started a parochial fund, every regular communicant subscribing to it each quarter any sum they liked, some a penny, some threepence, and some a half-crown. There were 286 members, and their subscriptions amounted to £380 in the four years. The benefit of this fund does not consist in the amount of

NEW SAINT AGATHA'S

money, but in the sense of having a stake in the parish, the possibility
of using with reality the word "my," as "my church," "my service,"
"my clergy." The number would have been increased, but in many
cases whole families are communicants, and the father would give for
all, or at any rate for his wife, even if the children who were in work
gave themselves.

Then the special funds were mostly collected in the parish; for a
poor scavenger who was killed, £130; for Mr. Osborne, when he left
us, £123; for the *Victoria* catastrophe, £114, the mothers giving up
their treat that year; in the parochial sales also, both in the buying
and selling departments, parishioners were largely represented. The
last fund that they collected, amounting to £100 14s. 6d. in six
months, was to buy a new altar for the church, and when, on leaving,
I asked them whether I might use this for paying off part of the
beautifying of the Lady Chapel, every subscriber but one willingly
gave me leave. If the widow, who cast her mite into the Treasury,
brought joy into the heart of the great Watcher of all men's deeds,
surely that heart has received joy over and over again in our poor
Landport slum, for His eye saw the self-denial entailed. There are
some who give that which costs them nothing. There are some who
give that which costs them their pleasure. There are some who give
that which costs them their daily bread. At that cost over and over
again many of our people have cast into the Treasury of God.

On the day before I left, and they had only been collecting about
three weeks, they gave me £175, making me promise to spend it upon
myself. I need not say the great Godsend it has been to me, for I left
S. Agatha's as poor as I went there, even poorer, for once, when in
dire necessity, I had to sell all my books. And so, as I am now without
salary or employment, I am living on that money. I remember their
generosity at every meal I eat, and every time I lie down in bed, and it
is a joy to me beyond all joys that I owe this, as very nearly all else
during this last ten years, to their love and forethought. For I still
have to be very busy. You will see by this account that I have a debt of
over £3000 to pay. I thought at one moment of his interview that the
Bishop would have said something about this debt, for I am paying
for the church in which I shall never minister again, for an increased
playground for the school in which I shall never teach again, for the

bad house next the parsonage, so that it may be enlarged, though I may never live there again, for an organ for the new church. And then there are some boys whom I am still bound to help, and one or two other cases, which I consider depend on me. At any rate, the practical question arises, the builder, the lawyer, and the architect must be paid. I am specially anxious about the builder. The head of the firm is just dead, and of necessity they must arrange business matters. They have been most upright and honourable, completing their business in a most satisfactory manner, I have overdrawn my bank account, I have borrowed from friends, I have even borrowed from money which was given me to spend upon myself, and by these means I have paid £800 more than I have received. I still owe them £1200. I am preaching ten courses of sermons a week this Lent to try and raise this money.

An old Wykehamist, overcoming his shyness, penetrated into the vestry of a church where I was preaching, and asked me if he could do anything for me. He had only just left school, so he could not give me money, but he proposed that his mother should get up a drawing-room meeting. Lord Encombe kindly came and took the chair, and Mrs. Burton sent me £58, the proceeds of the meeting. I think I am proudest of all that her servants, who hear me preach in London, all contributed to that result. A kind friend has taken the Pump-room at Tunbridge Wells, to give me an opportunity of lecturing, as well as preaching at S. Barnabas there. A lady is giving me her drawing-room in Chester Street early in May. I cannot take the holiday which I need so much, far less think of undertaking any new work, even if anybody would offer it me, until I have collected this £3000. And I am afraid that it will be very hard for me to get this money. The action of the Bishops of Durham and Worcester, and of the Rector of Croydon, not only prevent me getting money in these actual places (though I have just heard from the Vicar of Evesham, where the Bishop inhibited me, that the good people there, whom I have never seen, are going to send me their Lent savings), but have a tendency to prejudice me in the minds of other people. But I am sure if anybody would go down to see S. Agatha's, walk round the parish, examine our buildings, etc., they would discover that there has been no waste in our expenditure, and that we have taught our people not only to give, for they subscribe to all our funds, but, however mistaken I may be myself in my own opinions, to be loyal and dutiful members of the Church of England. Of course, if I had left after another two years there would have been no difficulty about the money; indeed, I do not think that, even if I had left at Easter, there would have been much. At any rate, everything that is there now belongs to the Church of England. The Bishop has approved of the priest-in-charge. If I wished it, I could not interfere in one single ceremony, or give one single instruction, and so I do think that, if there is anyone who admires our work, or thinks it has been useful and done good, now is the time that they should prove it by helping me to pay these debts. A meeting was once held to sympathise with a poor woman, who had lost her husband. Two gentlemen delivered very eloquent speeches, which drew tears from the eyes of those who heard them. The third speaker said, "I have no eloquence, but I sympathise £10," which he put down upon the table. The kindest things imaginable have been said about me by all sorts of people, and written in all sorts of papers. I am extremely grateful and gratified, but I think I should now appreciate a little of the other kind of speaking.

BALANCE SHEET

£	s.	d.
Central Wykehamist Committee		
11,292	3	0
Church Societies		
1,074	7	1
Diocese Societies		
759	12	6
Special Funds		
899	12	4
S. Agatha's Offertories		
3,032	13	11
Sales and Collections in Parish		
1,786	1	11
Profit of Shop		
646	1	0

Rents and Club Dues

499   4   11

Debts Repaid, and sums under £1

471   16   1

Winchester Houses

121   17   11

R. R. D.

313   7   0

Offertories, Meetings, Concerts, etc.

3,137   0   8

Anonymous Donations

6,428   1   9

Subscribers

17,352   14   8

Debt (for which Rev. R. R. Dolling is responsible)

3,090   0   0

_____

£50,904 14 9

_____

EXPENDITURE

£   s.   d.

Travelling

446   6   5

Postage, Stationery, Bank Charges

863   16   7

Clubs

984   3   7

Mission

5,530 18   0

Charity

3,258 13   8

Salaries

5,591 17   9

Chapel Expenses

1,317 10   7

Buildings Bought

5,325 14   1
Special Offertories
1,226 13   7
Penitentiary
1,360 9   0
Emigration
1,115 5   1
Building Schools
3,384 11   10
Sunday Schools
397   1   10
Special Funds
662   11   4
Building Parsonage
1,381 17   1
S. Agatha's Orphanage
4,500 0   0
New Church
11,308 11   4
Endowment
1,300 0   0
Remitted to J. G. Talbot, Esq., *re* New Church
948   13   0
_____

£50,904 14 9
_____

XIII.
Winchester.

In this book, which tries to tell of the Winchester College Mission, you will perhaps be disappointed that so little is said actually about Winchester; but that was the most distinctive part of their method; from first to last they never wanted to intrude. They put me in charge of the Mission, they paid me my salary, they entrusted me, as you will have seen, with large sums of money; but they never from first to last desired to dictate methods, or to hinder even when my methods were not quite at one with their own. It was an extraordinary generosity, and I am afraid that I have oftentimes put it to the test.

Placing the Mission at Landport was a stroke of genius on the part of the late Headmaster, Dr. Ridding. It enabled the men to become quite familiar with the work which was being carried on in their name. Prefects could come down from Saturday to Sunday night, and on leave-out days any man in the school could come down. Recently some change as to leave-out days has made this more difficult, but it is a matter of great congratulation to me that most of the elder men, both present and past, do not know the Mission merely by hearsay. Bedrooms were always kept ready for them, and I think, as a rule, they enjoyed themselves when they stayed with us, or, at least, they had the grace to appear to do so. When I speak of this, people always say, "What did they do?" I am afraid I have to answer, They did not do anything. Someone used to take them round the parish on Saturday night, and show them the different clubs, or they stayed in the gymnasium, or they came up to my own room and talked. Sometimes, if there was a great stress of work, they would help us in directing envelopes, or copying circulars. On Sunday they went to church, and took their meals with us - a plain breakfast of bread and butter, which we have to have on Sundays because so many breakfast with us, was never objected to by them; and the Sunday dinner was shared with thirty or forty other people, mostly of a different rank of life to which they were accustomed. Writing it down now in cold blood it does not seem anything, but I am sure it was everything - a liberal education, a discovery that all men are pretty much the same, that even the grossest sin, the direst poverty, has not the power of annihilating true manhood - above all the lesson that true worth consists not in what a man has, but what a man is; and perhaps they just guessed at the higher lesson that union with God is not only the power of a perfect cleansing, but the power of a renewed life, which renders him who possesses it true and beautiful. Of course, some men grasped all this easily, others saw things only as they were; but I do not believe that any man ever stayed with us who did not go away better for the visit.

I have been astonished oftentimes, when men came back long after they left school to stay with us how much more deeply such thoughts had penetrated their souls than I at the moment had believed. It seemed to them very difficult to realise that almost all our inmates were of what are called the lower, oftentimes of the degraded, classes; but men are strangely imitative, and our inmates naturally adopted the customs of those amongst whom they lived. The boy, too, of the lower class is generally wanting in self-consciousness. He talks freely and easily. The things he talks about are generally matters of experience to him. He seldom theorises. He is desirous of making those in his company feel at ease. I have seen Winchester men coming to us very anxious to condescend, to be polite, and I have seen them utterly nonplussed at the extraordinary good manners, simplicity, and powers of conversation of the fellows sitting round our table. Practically they came to teach, they remained to learn. I do not suppose that they were conscious of their intention, or of the result of their visit.

Then, too, their coming down gave me an opportunity of speaking plainer and straighter than I well could at Winchester. It was a great gain, having this opportunity with the leading men and heads of houses. It is very wonderful that they never seemed to resent this at all; sometimes I even flatter myself they liked it. They saw, too, the awful havoc which sin makes in character. Their lives at Winchester are so happy and so employed that they have little time or, perhaps inclination, to imagine the lives of those who are the very opposite of themselves, and, I think, seeing these lives did impress them very much. I judge this not only from what they said, but from the fact that several, I might say many, of them have privately helped me not only with money, but by taking pains in getting lads situations. And this interest has not been merely for a moment, just quickened by the sight of the poverty or distress, but has lasted after they left Winchester. Men did me even the honour of making me their confidant about themselves, or about some other man in the school for whom they were anxious. I grieve to-day, now that the chance has gone from me, over many opportunities wasted, sloth and pride so often preventing one, and one's own selfish nature continually supplying the excuse, "This is not the proper moment to speak," or, "You might lose your influence by speaking."

These days spent with me gave me the right to ask for hospitality in return. At first I only went to College, Joseph, my first Prefect of Hall, making this a very easy matter for me; and where Mrs. Richardson, the second master's wife, is, there can never be embarrassment. And so under her hospitable roof I began my venture of spending one day a week in Winchester. Then Harold Bilbrough, head of Mr. Kensington's house, asked me to go there. And soon the kind hospitality of the House Dons enabled me to visit every House in the school. I arrived in time to dine with the men in their hall. Then in the afternoon we watched cricket or football, or whatever was going on; in the winter the House Prefects giving me tea up at the House, in the summer ices, or an equivalent, at Louisa's. Alas! Louisa's is now no more; there is a school shop instead. The House Don usually asked four or five men in to dinner in the evening; sometimes I was asked to say a few words at *"Preces";* then the head of the House would take me into each gallery, and I saw all the fellows in bed, got to know, if possible, the younger ones, saw if there were any clothes I could take down to my people at home; a chance often arose of saying in jest a word that went deeper, or sometimes a word of comfort, but at any rate it broke down all shyness. I cannot for one single moment flatter myself that I exercised much influence, certainly not a religious influence strictly so-called. That was not my business. My religious mission was to Landport, not to Winchester, and I should have been utterly disloyal to the Winchester authorities and the parents of the boys if I had even tried to exercise such influence. On the other hand, I do believe that I was able to help many a man in the crisis of his school life, and to say many a word which would last after he left Winchester, and I judge from many letters received long after men have left the school, and from kind words which Dr. Fearon and the masters have said to me, that they thought the influence which I had at Winchester was really helpful to the school life.

Though it is difficult for me to speak of this, it is very easy for me to speak of the extraordinary help Winchester has been, personally, to me. The days spent there were days of perfect relaxation. In the summer watching cricket in Meads was a pure joy, one after another, men and Dons coming up to tell of all the news, and to discuss what was going on. There is, perhaps, no playing-field as beautiful in the whole of England; in front of you S. Catherine's Hill with its crown of trees, on one side the College Chapel, on the other S. Cross; everywhere gleams of beauty, and even on the sultriest day a delightful breeze. Then the most restful of all surroundings, a perfectly smooth green sward, and to give life the extraordinary excitement of the game, when the one thing that one desired most was that a man's batting or bowling in a foreign match should entitle him to get into Lord's; on the less sacred sward games innumerable, the anxiety of House captains about the younger men coming on, and dear Fort coaching and encouraging everybody. Beautiful as it all was, I am not sure that the intense excitement of Sixes or Fifteens, our Winchester football, was not even greater; the endeavour to fathom the mystery why commoners have a special go and *verve* of their own, the discussing it over and over again with House men and College men and with Dons. Sometimes people talk as if too much is made of games, that they are altogether Philistine, destroying refinement. At any rate, at Winchester this was never the case. From an experience of ten years, I would say that the vast majority of men in the Eleven and the Football teams were the nicest men in the school, and I have grown to know most of these men extremely well. My first year I did not; men were shy of me. Perhaps they thought that, because I was a parson, I was likely to be a "smug." But I remember well my second year, when the Captain of Lord's, I think it was Thesiger, walked arm in arm with me across Meads, I felt I had won a final victory. And the real beauty of the whole thing was, these men never guessed what they were doing for me. Their pure kindness was so modest, so unassuming, it was like eating and drinking new life. Age has nothing to do with years, the Winchester Missioner never can become an old man. Living amongst my own boys at home one did not gain this, there is so much of tears and sorrow, so much that is sordid mixed up in their lives, they are often so very old themselves. But to see these, one succeeding to another, ever young, ever enthusiastic, with literally no cares, and just as much work as was good for them, and to be allowed to enter into their life, to become part of the school, this rendered possible by their wonderful generosity, was to realise all the liberality of their environment and the beauty of their homes. I have come to Winchester oftentimes with a heart almost broken with sorrow; that heart-break has never lasted out one hour. Of course there is another side. We English deem that because a system suits eighty out of every hundred boys, it must suit the other twenty, and so the other twenty have to come to school. It is an atmosphere where they do not develop, where what is best and truest in them seems to be for ever driven back into their own hearts, until the best ceases to be good and sometimes becomes the worst - boys timid in will, weak in body, real cowards in spirit, they cannot help it. If parents, discovering such a one in their family, would devise some other method of education for them, it would be better for them and better for schools, for it is these boys who bring out in others whatever is vulgar and cruel, and there is latent vulgarity and cruelty in most boys from fourteen to sixteen. The best set of Prefect's eyes cannot be everywhere, and consequently little eyes are sometimes dimmed with tears, and little hearts are broken. And then there are bad boys. Take any four hundred men, women, or girls, and you will find bad ones amongst them. And badness has a strange way of impressing itself on others. Thank God, at that age it does not sink very deep, the bad is very superficial, and leaves little or no mark behind it. Oh, the blessed power of recovery in the young!

We have two great blessings at Winchester. We are a small school

- only four hundred - and none of our men are very rich. There is a perfect friendliness between all the masters and the men. Of course, I have heard words of anger against Dons, but I have never known a real hard thought about one of them. It is an extraordinary friendliness, and this friendliness passes down into the whole school. There are generations of brothers, coming one after the other, sometimes three in the same house at the same time, the greatest safeguard possible. And, above all, a deep, wholesome, religious spirit - not perhaps what would satisfy exact theologians, but manly and straightforward. For as I believe of my own children at Landport, so I believe of Winchester men. All that is necessary for the soul's salvation is all that it is necessary for a boy to learn - the power of prayer, the power of repentance, the power of the Sacraments, and these can be learned long before a boy comes to school - his mother the one priceless teacher. We need at school the opportunity of testing the religion learned, far more than of learning religion, and when the boy is equipped with the simple armour which I have spoken of, he is well prepared for every emergency of temptation. I remember a little lad once saying to me, when I saw him working late at night, "I am mugging John." I suppose when boys reach the sixth form they are intellectual enough to understand criticism, even of the Greek Testament; but I deprecate myself the Bible in any case being turned into a school book, and I think the parents who imagine that they can impose upon the schoolmaster their duty of teaching religion to-their children, inflict on their children a cruel wrong, on the master an impossible task.

I would I had the power to write what I feel about Winchester. I would I had words to make you feel how I have realised the magnificence of its great tradition - an unbroken chain of upright English gentlemen, holding the most useful place in their nation's history; not perchance the most brilliant, but certainly amongst the most dependable men of their time - and how earnestly I believe that this tradition is realised by almost every man in the school, and that the nation will realise it just as truly in times to come as in times past.

This intimate knowledge of men at school naturally led to my knowing many of their families, in Winchester language their "pitch-up"; and truly the Mission has discovered a new interpretation of that notion, if not perhaps its origin; for I think almost every family that I have known has contributed to the funds of the Mission, not only in money, but in clothes, in asking parties of us to spend the day with them, sometimes even in supporting cases that we were very anxious about. It has led, too, to a kind of association of prayer for the Mission's welfare, composed of relatives of past and present Wykehamists. Miss Wigram, of South Lodge, Champion Hill, S.E., the sister of " The Cat" and " The Kitten," would be glad to give particulars.

Once or twice a year, too, I was able to go up to Oxford, sometimes to Cambridge, and thus keep in touch with the men there. There is something especially charming in this hospitality, though I doubt if one could stand it for very long, unless one could discover the curious secret of Mr. Lucraft. There is perhaps nothing more attractive than seeing a man act host for the first time, especially when he has got the kitchens and plate-closet of Magdalen behind him. I remember on one visit a distinguished Low Church clergyman suddenly asking me what I had been doing for the spread of religion, and I could only answer, "Taking three square meals a day." I think he was very much shocked; but you will likely understand that under this hospitality there was hidden a true generosity, and an interest in the Mission and myself. New College was naturally my head-quarters, and men took really extraordinary pains to arrange that I should see as many Wykehamists as possible at the different centres of hospitality, and I have always thought that taking trouble, certainly at Oxford, was the greatest proof of taking real interest. God, too, allows one to speak more plainly at Oxford than one could at Winchester, and there come into my memory now many conversations full of the deepest interest. At any rate, it is a great privilege to have won the right to speak, even if men did not always follow the advice given, and letters received years after the conversation - many received since men knew that I was leaving Landport - almost induce me to flatter myself that the Mission has been a much greater help than at the time I ever realised. Of course, it is natural that men who knew me at Winchester should have some interest in the Mission, one would have been disappointed if they had not; but to discover that a large number of old Wykehamists were cordially ready to befriend us, not only with money, but with sympathy, was a very astonishing revelation to me. The larger part of the money has come from them; and when you think that it was given into the hands of a socialistic Ritualist to use and to distribute, you can measure something of the generosity. It would not be becoming for me to mention names, but if this book falls into the hands of men who have been on the Committee, especially the Treasurers and Secretaries for the last ten years, I would like them to realise how their loyalty to us has been one of the chief factors in a generous Wykehamical support, which gave us the grace of perseverance in the most difficult time of our work. I am conscious, as no one else can be, how often my own actions have strained this loyalty. I know that not only old Wykehamists, but even the school authorities themselves, have often been very severely tried by things we have deemed it our duty to say or to do. Sometimes a word in a letter, or reading between the lines, might suggest caution to us, but never during the whole of these ten years has any single word been said by anyone in authority, or by others who had gained the right by having contributed to our funds, that could be construed into any other meaning than the tenderest love and the truest desire to help. Perhaps there could be no greater sign of that real liberalism that permeates every true Englishman, in whatever camp, either political or religious, circumstance may have placed him. To Wykehamists at Oxford or Cambridge, to men in the City and at the Bar, to soldiers scattered throughout the world, and to priests working at home and abroad, to schoolmasters, Indian civilians, and to Bishops, I, who have failed in my endeavour to do some work for Winchester, venture to offer my heartiest thanks for innumerable acts of kindness and generosity during these ten years.

XIV.
Our Method of Services.

I HOPE through all this description of social work at Landport, Winchester, Oxford, and elsewhere, you have been able to read a deeper truth than mere Socialism even at its best. The lesson which is the foundation of all work like ours is that, however earnestly you may strive to change circumstances, you must realise that change of character is the thing to be aimed at, and practically if you do not achieve this, you have hardly achieved anything at all. And I know but one method by which this change of character can be effected, the method of Jesus Christ, not merely to show to people the perfection and beauty of His character - that oftentimes might lead only to despair - but to enable them, by the means which He Himself has ordained,, to be partakers of His very nature. To say to a poor sin-ruled creature, whom you know all his old companions, every public-house door as it swings open, will allure into the ways of sin again, "Be like Jesus, be good," is only making a demand that you yourself know can never be fulfilled. But to be able to say to him, "Here is this Jesus, Who for your sake became a real man, as you are a man, Who worked in the carpenter's shop, earning, with the sweat of His brow, daily bread for Himself, His dear mother, and her husband, Who was disappointed and injured by His friends as well as by His enemies, Who was really tempted by the devil, Whose life in many respects was just like your own, Who never turned away His face from any poor wretched outcast, but spoke to them tenderly and gently words of love and hope, Who when He could do no more for you by way of example, willed to die for you: having nothing else to give, He gave His own life-blood, and in the giving of that, won for you a power of union with Himself, that though you must do your part, and be sorry for your sins, and try to be better, He will as surely do His part by letting His precious blood wash away your sin, and strengthen you to live an amended life. Here is this Jesus standing as it were between the living and the dead, so few, few living, so many, many dead, dead with a death more terrible far than the worm and corruption can effect, for they but touch the outward covering of a man, with a death which has destroyed the real life, the knowledge that God was their Father, that they had souls capable of everything that was beautiful and true. Here is Jesus, Who can give even to the clumsy vulgar body the power of doing gracious acts, of speaking true words, Who can give to the intellect the power of realising true noble ideals, and so assimilating them, that they may become a very fibre of their thoughts." In almost all our people there was this death, this living, hopeless, faithless death. Who could deliver them from the body of this death? One Who could restore to them faith in the supernatural, hope in themselves, love towards their fellow-men. No preaching can do this. I believe nothing can but the Blessed Sacrament. The compassion, which Jesus learned in the trials of His life, taught Him to realise that man, if he is to be touched, must be touched in his entirety, that an attempt to deal with him spiritually alone is bound to fail. How Christ-destroying is all that theology that tries to be wiser and more spiritual than the Christ! The Blessed Sacrament is not only the prolongation of the Incarnation in the world, but it is a means by which Jesus wills that He shall be apprehended by the multitude. And so ten and a half years ago I set before myself this as the method of my ministry. Some I know make the Blessed Sacrament the crown of their religion. I desired to make it the foundation as well. As the Incarnation is the revelation to us of God the Father, so the Divine Son wills to be known in the breaking of bread.

How far we succeeded in this, the following letter from Father Maturin will show:

"ST. ANDREW'S, N.B.,
"April , 1896.

"MY DEAR DOLLING,
"The wrench from S. Agatha's must be a great one for you, and I deplore it very much. For I had exceptional opportunities of seeing

behind the scenes into the real work, and its effects upon the people, during the mission which Robinson and I gave there a few months ago. Some things have left an impression upon my mind which I shall never, I think, quite forget.

"One was the extraordinary simplicity and reality of the people's worship. I do not think I have ever seen anything quite like it in the Church of England, though I have had a rather exceptionally wide experience of different parishes in England and America. The stiffness and formalism which haunts us and hampers us everywhere, was not known at S. Agatha's. You somehow succeeded in laying that ghost, and in teaching the people that the church is their home, where they should behave as if they are at home. Men came and went there as to a place of rest which they loved. Some time ago the Archbishop of Canterbury, and other bishops, made a move to have the churches left open for private prayer, but the people seldom use them. Somehow at S. Agatha's they do use their church; it had the appearance of being homelike and in constant use. I have often gone into some of our best-known churches in London in the daytime, and felt chilled and lonely, I have a very vivid memory of two occasions, amongst others, at S. Agatha's - one was a Saturday during the mission, when I had to go over to Southampton, and coming back in the afternoon I went straight to the church, and found many people in the church on their knees, and a constant stream of people coming and going. The other occasion was your last day at S. Agatha's. I got there late in the evening, and found a large congregation saying their own prayers, no service, and the people seeming to feel no need of help, but knowing themselves how to lay their needs before God. I shall never forget that devout congregation kneeling in perfect stillness in the dark church, having apparently learnt that lesson so hard to teach, especially to those who can't read, how to pour out their souls to God. It was the same at the Masses and other services; the people seemed to know how to pray.

"If you ask me to what this quite exceptional power of prayer is to be attributed, I think I can say without hesitation that, so far as I could judge, I should trace it to two things:

"(i.) One is your constantly keeping up their interest in all that was going on amongst them, by telling them of the needs and troubles of others, and suggesting prayers, extempore and others, to them. I could feel myself its power, and the way in which the people appeared to have grown used to bringing their own and others' difficulties constantly before God. Rigidity had to bend and yield before this, and it did, and real personal devotion took its place. At the same time the regular services in no sense lost any of their dignity. I have never seen a more dignified and devout Mass anywhere.

"(ii.) The other cause to which I attribute so much of the spirit of prayer, and the chief one, was that the people, however poor and ignorant, seemed to have a grasp upon, and a love of the Blessed Sacrament such as I have seldom, if ever, seen elsewhere. Their worship and their Christian life centred round it. You had wholly banished from their minds the idea that the Presence was only confined to the act of communion. It was enough for them to know the Blessed Sacrament was upon the altar, to crowd to the church - that attraction which draws Christendom was exercising its full sway over them, and the result was what one would expect. I feel convinced by what I saw, that we shall never get people to realise the Real Presence in all its fulness without reservation. The poorest at S. Agatha's 'knew what they worshipped.'

"No doubt along with all this there must have been careful and thorough teaching, but of that I will not speak. Only one other thing I will notice, though I might speak of many things. I was very much struck with the very extraordinary conversions. Some of those who had led very bad lives a few years before, appeared to have broken from the past in a way I have seldom seen before, and in the place of vice and degradation there was an extraordinary refinement; the past seemed gone. I have some cases especially in my mind at this moment. I believe - indeed, I have no doubt - this was owing in part, at least, to the fact that probably these poor people had never resisted; for they had never had the offer of the grace of the Sacraments, and with the first waking of conscience came the blessing of the knowledge of the Catholic Faith in its fulness. I should like to have taken some of those who criticise any departure from rigid conformity to Prayer Book methods, to see what I saw. Certainly no good results would justify anything that is wrong, but I conceive

that, so far as I could see, the methods of S. Agatha's were no greater
a departure from Prayer Book ways than is used, I suppose, in the
vast majority of parishes in England.

"But I must not write more. I only hope that S. Agatha's may go
on for the future upon the lines so well and so prayerfully laid down.

"Ever affectionately yours,

"B. W. Maturin."

Dr. Linklater built a very fitting Mission Church; it seated about
five hundred people, and I found Celebrations on Sunday at seven
and eight, morning and evening prayer, and a children's service; and
on week-days, Celebrations twice a week, and evensong every night, I
felt that it would be wiser to leave the Sunday services unchanged for
two years, supplementing them if I saw it was needed. But the
weekday services I took in hand very soon after I came. For my
brother priests and for my workers, it was very soon necessary to
have a daily Celebration, not only for the nourishment of our own
souls, but to give us the opportunity of pleading that Sacrifice for the
whole body of Christ's Church, and especially for the wants of our
own district. I say it with the fullest confidence, that this daily
Celebration has been the chief strength of the parochial life.

But here, at the very outset, we were met by the difficulty of that
rubric about three communicants, which seems to have become the
shibboleth which proves loyalty or otherwise to the Church of
England. Our numbers made it almost impossible for us to arrange
for three communicants each morning, even if I could
conscientiously have done this. I am told that there are churches
which qualify for saying a daily Mass by arranging that three people
will be responsible for each morning in the week. I can understand
few customs that are so likely to injure souls. Very soon one and
another beside the clergy and helpers began to drop in. Remember,
the poor have no room where they can pray alone. The church
becomes for them the customary place where prayer is to be made,
except the very brief morning and evening prayer. The Celebrations,
too, were offered on the different mornings with different intentions.
Soldiers, sailors, and emigrants one morning, Penitentiary work
another, and so on. Often the silent tears trickling down a woman's

face would show you she was praying for her own boy or her own girl. To these poor feeble folk, with no power of prayer or concentration of mind, with but few words which they can use, even in their daily intercourse, the knowledge that their just saying "Jack" or "Mary" as they knelt in silence, was the truest intercession, gathering all the sighs and tears of their heart in union with that all-sufficient Sacrifice, which alone could bring joy and peace to Jack or Mary. I had a better right to know this, for often as I went up into the vestry a name would be whispered in my ear, or a little piece of paper pressed into my hand. I think when I first told this to Bishop Thorold, he feared it was a kind of superstition, but when I could assure him that this grace of prayer gained before the Blessed Sacrament became the custom of the whole life, he no longer thought that we were making a superstitious use of it, or were training people to trust so in this great gift of God that they could not realise His presence elsewhere.

Soon, too, we found it necessary to arrange a special place for communicants. We had been able from the first to exercise a great deal of discipline in the parish. Remember the Church of England is the only religious body which exercises no discipline about Holy Communion. Of course, a great deal can be said on the side of the liberty of the communicant, and his being the best judge of his worthiness to receive. But surely something may be said on the other side, the duty of the priest to consider the Blessed Sacrament as a great trust. Practically I am sure it is a great hindrance to the authority of the Church among large numbers of people. Over and over again, in talking to earnest Nonconformists, they have expressed to me their wonder and amazement that we, who profess to honour the Blessed Sacrament so much, should actually take no pains to see it is not profaned. Their admirable system of letters of commendation at once puts the new-comer in communication with their church authorities, and it enables those authorities to judge about the man's fitness for Communion. I received a curious letter bearing upon this from an earnest Christian the other day. "When I was young and strong I devoted myself to organising in certain fields of philanthropy. I was a Churchman, and I taught both in the Sunday Schools of Conformity and Nonconformity. It will seem to you, perhaps, terribly lax, but I saw no valid reason why I should not

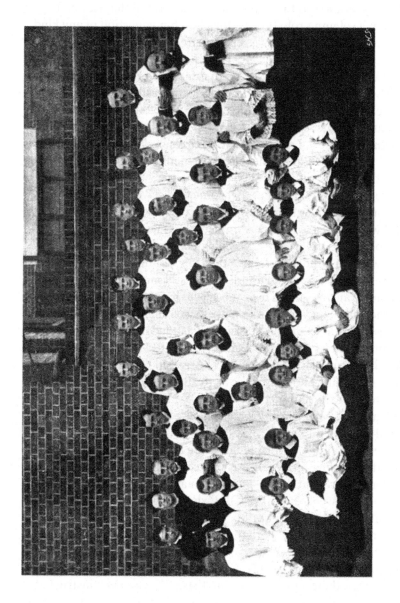

OUR CHOIR AND ACOLYTES

communicate in the chapel as well as regularly in my parish church. Before I was allowed to attend Communion at the chapel, I had to undergo a solemn probation. At the church no question of any kind was put to me, my fitness was entirely treated as either my own affair or a matter of indifference." At any rate, I am perfectly sure of this, that it would be fatal in a Mission district to offer the Sacraments freely without fencing them round with all possible discipline.

There is another great inconvenience in not knowing the number of communicants; sometimes too many Hosts are consecrated, sometimes too few. I suppose that three week-day mornings out of the six we had no communicants. It seemed to me, therefore, a perfectly profane thing to invite people to receive the Communion, to turn round and say "to them that come to receive the Holy Communion," when I knew no one was coming, most solemn, nay, awful words, then to allow my minister to make confession, perhaps the most grave and weighty possible in language, "in the name of all those who are minded to receive the Holy Communion," when he and I knew that no one was so minded, and, still more profane, to pronounce an absolution over those who have made no confession, or if they have, had no right to make that confession. Thus one set of rubrics and prayers in the Prayer Book landed me on the horns of a dilemma; either I was compelled to say what I knew was a mockery, or to give up my daily celebration. Ninety-nine clergymen out of a hundred, finding another rubric as to giving notice of Communion and another exhortation a difficulty, get rid of the difficulty by disregarding the rubric and by leaving the exhortation unsaid. Why should I not do the same?

The same kind of difficulty had to be faced with regard to the week-day evening service. It was wretchedly attended, and I do not wonder. We are told that in pre-Reformation times people came readily to the week-day offices. But what proof have we of this? Was the daily office, of which our Matins and Evensong is a survival, ever frequented by the laity? Perhaps people will answer that there is no obligation for the laity to go to church on a week-day, though the obligation has from the earliest days, I believe, been binding on the clergy to say their offices. Therefore these offices were constructed for the use of the clergy. But in a Mission district, where the people are practically heathen, and where you have little chance of instructing them except in church, the service of necessity must be such that they can join in it with edification. I believe you want two kinds of worship - one very dignified and ornate, which enables them to realise that they are making an offering to the Lord of Heaven and Earth, the other very simple and familiar, that they are talking to a loving Father Who knows all their needs and wants to help them. If you had the ornate worship alone, there would be a danger of mere ritualism. If you had the familiar worship alone, there might be a danger of what some people seem to be so unnaturally afraid of - too much familiarity. At any rate, saying Evensong every night, you would certainly have neither of the dangers, but, on the other hand, you would have none of the educational or heart-touching power, I am not venturing to make any suggestion about churches except such as those in my own district. But when we had said evening prayer to empty benches for a year, we thought the thing was hopeless. People would come to a prayer meeting in the Mission room, or in one of our own rooms, but they would not come to church, which was the very place where we wanted to get them. But directly we began a prayer meeting in church many people came, and God granted to us such visible proofs - His answer seen by all the people - that many times during the year, because we have continued the prayer meetings on Monday ever since, people would come with some special need, quite sure that, in some way or another, God would answer it. The Bishop of Guildford made it a strong point in his endeavour to arrange matters with the Bishop of Winchester that we should give up this extempore prayer, but I would rather have left the Mission than done so.

Then on Thursdays we began the Vespers of the Blessed Sacrament. This Bishop Harold Browne also objected to till he had read it, and then he said it was one of the most beautiful and scriptural services he had ever seen. I expect a good deal of ecclesiastical troubles might be stopped if Bishops would see things before they condemned them. The same psalms being always sung in the Vespers, the antiphon drawing out, as it were, the sacramental meaning of the psalm, was a wonderful education; the cope, the acolytes, and the incense, added a great dignity, a dignity which, at S.

Agatha's, has never been stilted or unnatural; and the impress of this
act of solemn worship upon many an ignorant heart left a true sense
of the dignity of worship and a glimpse of the supernatural. Those
who can read little, learn through ear and eye. These psalms, too,
have been a great heritage to many of our people. I have known many
a pain-stricken one recite them over and over again, a grace which
certainly would never have been gained by saying different psalms
every evening. And no one who has ever seen them at S. Agatha's can
doubt the power of the Stations. As I sit thinking now, I have not the
courage to speak of them; but Friday after Friday they were like a
great sob going up from the heart of this sinful place, to tell Jesus
how sorry we were that we had been His very murderers, driving the
thorns into His head, and the nails into His hands and feet. The
objection to Compline, that the congregation absolved the priest, was
so strangely ignorant, that the Bishop withdrew it at once. Thus our
week-day services took their present form, which have continued the
last eight years, with generally a little sermon added. The common
people always hear gladly.

Very soon the difficulty about the children pressed upon us. They
certainly had no conception of reverence or of worship. After much
prayer and consideration, I determined that the only solution was to
have a Children's Mass. I wonder if any parish priest has ever been
blessed with such Sunday School teachers as I have; many had taught
for Dr. Linklater; and though I don't think they liked me at all at first
- they thought I was very rough and severe - they loyally stuck to me.
At first, when we spoke of the Children's Mass, many of them seemed
to object to it; but a year's hard work had well prepared the children
for it. I was permitted to use the book in use at St. Alban's, Holborn,
and so got rid of that awful difficulty of inattentive children, for in
this book they are employed from the time they come into church till
they go out, either listening to the priest in those parts of the service
which he says aloud, or, while he is saying his private devotions,
being led by some responsible person in their own. What wonderful
services these have been. How they have trained boys and girls
naturally to come on to Communion. How they have impressed every
child with the dignity and solemnity of worship. How they have
taught them to realise God and the supernatural. And almost all this

is due to the devotion of the teachers. It is invidious, perhaps, to mention names, but all the teachers will understand why dear Barratt's name and Miss Damerum's come to my mind; they stand as a kind of representatives of the rest. And, if I might add one special parochial benefit, the Children's Mass gave us the first idea of the congregation singing their own Mass, for the children had no choir, and yet they sang Creed, Gloria, Benedictus, Agnus, everything.

This giving the children a service of their own mercifully got rid of them from Matins at 11 o'clock. Soon the older people, coming in at the end of the children's service, began to ask why they could not have the same kind of service. There were, however, two difficulties in the way. I felt bound to make no alteration in the morning and evening services on Sundays until I had been in the parish for two years. What a blessed probation this was, for it gave us time to train choir, acolytes, and congregation. When I told the original choir that they would have to go out of the chancel, which was very small and confined, and virtually sit in a corner, and that there would be a Celebration instead of Matins, they nearly all objected to the alteration. I am afraid I had tried them very much before; I always have been very hard on choirs. I had made them give up singing Gregorians - I never yet heard congregational Gregorians. Then when Major Foote kindly joined the choir, when he was stationed at Portsmouth, and tried to teach them proper tune, etc., with one accord they suggested that they could not learn to sing right, and he must accommodate his singing to theirs. I am afraid, as I have said, I was very hard on them, and not nearly patient enough. So we had to get a new choir ready when they would leave, train a set of acolytes, and teach the congregation. Nothing is more fatal than to introduce any change which people do not thoroughly understand. On Sunday nights, after Evensong, most of the congregation used to remain behind. I showed them all the vestments one by one, I made them follow in the Prayer Book every word of the service, I made them learn, to two easy settings of the Holy Communion, all the parts they had to sing, and this without any choir, I also explained to them all about the incense. I made them, either in rows, or individually, stand up and answer questions to show that they understood. At first, of course, they were shy, but Blind Willie, who, one might almost say,

COMMUNICANTS' LEAGUE, 1895

was divinely taught in these things, began by answering, and the others soon followed. We have never given up this habit of catechising, and so every change in worship has been well understood by the whole congregation. Some of our first acolytes have gone away from Portsmouth, some have married and given their place to others, some, like dear George Norton, are still upon the altar. Surely no place has ever been served like S. Agatha's. Their wonderful simplicity, their utter want of mannerism, not a ritualist amongst them all. From the first we had given out notice that no one could receive Communion at the children's service unless they had previously given in their names. This we had done in anticipation of the Sunday when Matins should be said at 9 o'clock, and the Holy Eucharist become the central act of our worship. No one had given in their names on that first Sunday morning, so we did not expect any communicants. But, while the children's service was going on, three smartly-dressed ladies came in, and, not content to kneel like other people at the bottom of the church until that service was over, pushed their way up amongst the children, whispering and looking about, to the utter amazement of the children, who judged from their teachers that it was utterly impossible that a grown-up person could behave badly in church. Seeing them in the front pew before the service began at 11, I ventured to ask them why they had come, and they said they had heard that this was such a curious church that they would like to see it, and that they were going to receive the Holy Communion. I found that they had come from close to S. Jude's Church. I saw by their manners that our church would disconcert them very much, and certainly not help them in preparing for a good Communion, so I whispered to the verger to get a cab, and, as soon as it came, I said, "It will be much better for you to make your Communions at S. Jude's, as you have not given me notice." So I walked down the church with them, put them into the cab, and paid the driver. Luckily this story got repeated, and that, together with the discomfort of the church, has largely kept sightseers away. Perhaps you will think I was very severe upon these ladies, but I am sure it was one of the most useful lessons I have ever given, both to them and to my people as well. Nothing can be so bad as going to a church because we hear that the preaching or the service is curious. One such person mars the whole atmosphere of religion, and, above all, I was anxious to keep Southsea people away, except those who worshipped with us from conviction.

Soon we added a dignity to the Evensong by vesting the officiant in a cope, and offering incense at the Magnificat. But I think I can say that there have been no changes in the services or ritual of S. Agatha's during the last eight years, except that we have added services for men and women alone, a second Celebration daily, and an extra one on the first Sunday in the month, and evening prayer daily at 6.30; so that when we went into our new church we had five services daily, eight services every Sunday, and ten on the first Sunday in the month.

During the winter, too, late at night, so as to catch the impossibles, my dear friend Hobbs, chief schoolmaster on the *Vernon*, enabled us to give a magic-lantern service, which was extremely valuable.

Very largely, too, we have been helped in all this by our blind organist, dear Richard Whittick. There is a wonderful tenderness in the sympathetic touch of a blind player, and he has given a note of refinement to the whole of our services, playing on the worst organ that ever was built, and yet bringing music out of it. The services made a great demand upon him, because we required him almost every night, and so it was very lucky for him that Mr. Attree, the organist of the Dockyard Church, relieved him on Thursday evenings, and at two of the Sunday services. We owe to Mr. Attree many of the beautiful photographs with which this book is illustrated. By the way, among the other things I have to pay, though I only had the use of it for six weeks, is £225 to Messrs. Hill for our new organ. Perhaps it is to our present choir that my greatest apologies are due, for they have quite willingly altogether effaced themselves, content merely to lead the congregation, and to have whatever music and hymns I thought best. And yet we all felt that in moving into a new church the choir needed strengthening, and so, when dear Mr. Roe left us because his health had broken down, God sent the Reverend Stanley Gresham, the exact man we needed. "With the boys and the choirmen he really did wonders, and he is only just another instance, if we needed one, how from September, 1885, till January, 1896, we have never lacked either the persons or the things which we needed. There were ninety-nine communicants on our first Easter Sunday, and over five hundred on our last Easter Sunday. "Increase Celebrations, encourage non-communicating attendance, and you will lessen the number of communicants." How often this is said. Let S, Agatha's answer it. "Teach too much about the Blessed Sacrament, give people an exaggerated belief about it, and you will train them to neglect other church services; their objective worship will destroy their subjective faith in God." Let S. Agatha's answer. "Have all these ornate services, increase this ritualism, press confession, and you will alienate the lay people, and drive worshippers away from their own church." Let S. Agatha's answer. For ten years we have taught and encouraged non-communicating attendance. Our communicants had outgrown our Mission Church. We had taught practically nothing else but that the Blessed Sacrament is the revelation of Christ, Who is the revelation of the Father. Not only our Eucharists but our other services were filled to overflowing, and faith in Christ as a personal Saviour, and the Father as a personal Providence, had permeated the whole of our parish. For ten years we have taught confession, heard confessions openly in church, for eight years we have had all these ritualistic services, and though five times the Bishop of the Diocese has seen fit to summon us to his presence, and to remonstrate with us upon some practice or doctrine, yet no single complaint has ever been made by one person in our parish.

XV.
Our Method of Religion.

Of course, the actual church services must, in every well-ordered parish, be supplemented by a considerable amount of religious work outside the church, and our first object being to make Communion a real bond of union between us all, we strove by Bible Classes, and by private instruction, to either prepare for Confirmation, or, if people had already been confirmed, to restore them to their privileges. I differ, I know, from many of my brethren about the age of Confirmation. Very seldom has anyone been presented at S. Agatha's under fourteen, and I should think that more than half of those confirmed were over twenty, many of them much older. The preparation took about four months each year, the lady-workers taking the girls and young women, I the married women, and my assistant clergy sharing with me the boys and men. Classes had often to be held at half-past nine, and even later, our younger people worked so late. It was possible to weed out a great many during the first two months, those who could but would not attend, and those who, though attending, showed by their manner that they had no real interest in it. I am sure it was far better to repress rather than over-encourage, and if there was any grit or desire, those who were refused were bound to offer themselves next year. It was of the utmost importance for their mates and companions not to make it too cheap. The individual work, if it was only ten minutes a week, was infinitely more precious than all classes, and then there were the three final preparations in church, of which I have spoken before. We never made confession compulsory - I do not think that it would be honest in the Church of England to do so - and though instances occurred in which one was sorry one could not, and believed that it would have been greatly to the benefit of the candidate, yet, on the other hand, one realised the great danger it would have been if it had been forced, and therefore not really natural. On the whole, I am inclined to believe that the voluntary system in this, as in most other things, is really the best. It is wonderful what experience these Confirmation seasons gave to us. Last night I was preaching at Kennington, and the parish priest told me, "The people here say that you seem to know all about them and their lives." I am quite sure all this knowledge came from my Confirmation work at Landport. There is a simplicity and naturalness in people without any veneer of society, so that, when they trust you, they will literally tell you anything about themselves, and very often those who, when they first came to us, would have scoffed at the idea of making a confession, practically made their confessions long before they formally did so.

We had ten Confirmations during my time, and 580 people were confirmed. And here you will see that the great difficulty of a parish like ours, and one of its chief sorrows, are the migratory habits of the population, especially amongst the men; 46 of these have become soldiers and sailors, 38 have been emigrated, 141 have left the town, 30 have moved too far away from the church to remain communicants with us, and 40 are dead. Thus more than half have passed away from our immediate influence, and no longer strengthen the parochial life. Of the 285 who remain, 46 have lapsed altogether from Communion, 37 are irregular communicants, about three or four times a year, and 202 are members of the Communicants' League, most of them communicating once a month. It is over these lapsed ones that we sorrow most, and there come up before one's mind, now that one has no further chance with them, so many wasted opportunities. It is only God Who is never hopeless about any single soul, but Whose divine excuse, "They know not what they do," is said continually for even the most sinful in the moments of their greatest depravity. I am sure that if we could only have translated into our ministry something of this hope, this excuse, I should not have to write the awful words, "46 lapsed," and yet, thank God, the judgment of their having lapsed is only our judgment, not His, and perhaps He might write over us, that if we were only more honest we would have lapsed too. Remember, nothing in their surroundings urges them towards religion. How many of us, especially the clergy, are religious because we needs must. Many of those who have gone away write to us continually, and we know all about them, but, except by their prayers, they can no longer strengthen S. Agatha's. If all these had stayed our Easter Communion would have been over eight hundred instead of five hundred. The following letter just received will show how a boy we prepared for Confirmation fulfilled his obligations:

"SYDNEY, N.S.W.,
"February 11th, 1896.

"DEAR FATHER DOLLING,

"After a very long silence, I again write these few lines to you, hoping to find you in good health; and also to let you know that I am still alive and well, and (thanks to your kind teaching) I am living a sober and quiet life, and have done so since I came out here. But I should very much like to see you again, and also dear old S. Agatha's. I am making Melbourne my home when I am on shore, and I attend Christ Church, South Yarra (Canon Tucker). Do you know him? He is a good man. I have quite lost sight of W---. I think that he must either be dead or gone home again. The times are getting better out here, as there are thousands of people flocking to the West Australian gold-fields. But they die there by hundreds. I want to ask you one favour. I should like to have one of your cabinet photos like you used to sell at the shop. Do send me one. So now I think I must draw to a close. With kind regards to all and best wishes,

"I remain, yours faithfully,

"W. H. L--- ."

And here is a letter about a boy whom we emigrated three years ago, about whom we were extremely doubtful, but who has done so well that he is trying to emigrate his family.

"EAST END EMIGRATION FUND,
"March 26th, 1896.

"Dear Sir,

"You will be glad to hear that I received the following report from our agent in Montreal with reference to this family:-

" 'I went three times to Bluebonnets to see Stigant before I met him. He married a few months ago; he and his wife seem very happy and comfortable. He has only two rooms at present, but has rented a good house for the 1st May. He is quite confident he can procure work for Stevens and his brothers on arrival. He seems an earnest, steady fellow, and I think his people will get along very well with him. They might come on the first ship, arriving here about May 1st.'

"I feel sure that you will be glad to hear this satisfactory report of young Stigant.

"Yours truly,

"Walter Barratt."

I do not suppose that anyone considers that the Tractarian movement, in its later developments, has been a pure gain to the Church of England. I can remember, when I was a lad, a week's preparation for the monthly Communion, in which all the family shared, the mentioning of it at daily family prayer, the putting off of engagements during the week, the private talks both with my father and my mother, and thanksgiving at family prayer the night after. We who talk so condescendingly of the past have very grievous need to ask ourselves whether, while religion has increased, piety has decreased; and whether the multiplication of weekly communicants really and truly means better Communions, and does not often mean a Communion without preparation before, and without thanksgiving after. God forbid I should say that this is the case, but we all know that every privilege entails an increased responsibility, and that the body is in danger just as much from over, as from undernourishment, unless that nourishment be perfectly assimilated to the whole system. At any rate, I endeavoured to keep this thought before me when planning our only parochial society, which we called our Communicants' League. It was unique, at any rate, in one respect: it had no rules. I have so oftentimes found, in hearing confessions, how burdensome the rule becomes even of saying a daily collect, and there is nothing more fatal to the progress of the soul, especially to the timid soul, than incurring unnecessary responsibilities, I believe that no member of the League ever passed a day without thinking of S. Agatha's, and oftentimes among the ignorant, who have so little power of expressing themselves, thoughts are the best prayers. But the League had four suggestions: first, to be present at Mass every Sunday; secondly, to prepare for Communion on the first Sunday in the month, if conscience taught, to go to confession, and, if possible, making the Communion; thirdly, to make it fasting, if possible; fourthly, to contribute something to the expenses of the parish every quarter, the sum being left wholly to the conscience of the contributor. None of these rules were obligatory, but they were almost universally kept, except as regards making the Communion, because some only came to Communion once in two months. In order that there might be no difficulty about the preparation, there were services on Mondays, for women alone, at 3 p.m.; on Wednesdays, for lads, at 9 p.m.; on Thursdays, for girls, at 9 p.m.; a general preparation of conscience, for women, at 8 p.m. on Fridays, for men at 8 p.m. on Saturdays; and I sat in church practically the whole of the last four days of the week to hear confessions. The preparation of conscience was very valuable. I said aloud a commandment, then asked eight or ten questions about it, making a little pause after each question; beyond getting drunk, doing wrong as they call it, and stealing, the poor have very little knowledge of what sin is. This system of examination prepared many for their first confessions. The League has 441 members. On the first Sunday in the month everybody gives their name as they come into church, and their Communions are marked in a book. We are able thus to test their attendance, and also mark change of address, a very important matter in a migratory parish. The League was responsible, also, for the Day of Perpetual Intercession, of which I have spoken, and for a service for men alone on Sunday afternoons.

Once a year, in S. Agatha's week, we kept a great festival, when we all supped together, anyone sending what they liked in the way of food. Sometimes there was too much, though our appetites were generally good. Sometimes we had not enough. But that was all part of S. Agatha's system. At these meetings the whole of the secrets of the parish for the coming year were disclosed. How splendid our great gymnasium used to look, filled with tables covered with all kinds and sorts of things, the most curious puddings, the most extraordinary cakes, in the funniest plates and dishes. Such an intense union and harmony amongst us all. Even when I had to say, as I often had, hard, really hard, things, with what love, what tenderness, were they accepted. I, at any rate, shall never see the like again, for it is seldom granted twice to a man in his life to be called to a work like this, for they were all, in the truest sense, my own children; I had begotten them nearly all in Jesus Christ, and they have proved their loyalty not, I thank God, to me, but to our common Master. When I had to leave, all our farewells were said in church. During those last few days, when they saw us in the street, they went within doors themselves. And yet, with all that, not one was absent from their duty to the priest who came to take temporary charge. No single one said, "Because Mr. Dolling has left, I leave." They knew their duty was to Christ and His Church, not to me. And yet it was a very grievous trial to them, so grievous that, to many of them, it almost meant shipwreck. I think I am committing no breach of confidence if I let you read one or two of the letters which I received just after I left.

"DEAR FATHER,

"I went to church on Friday night no stations of the cross. I went on Sunday it looked nice to see the Bishop their for he looked like us very much cut up. our text was Jesus weep and God shall wipe away all tears from every eye. it do not matter were we look weather up high or down low the very bricks seem to say you cannot do without him but we are all going to be very good to this father because he speaks so good of you so you mast make haste and get better. I hope Misses Dolling are better.

"I remain yours truly."

The Bishop referred to is the Bishop of Southwell.

"DEAR MR. DOLLING,

"You didn't come to see me before you went, and my heart was too full to come and see you. I have not been to Church yet, for I have been very poorly, for this job have pretty nigh broke me up altogether, after sitting under you for ten years, and never have been inside another church nor chapel since, and I hope the Bishop won't close his eyes to go to sleep till he sends you back again, for I can't sleep, and I don't see for why he should, but, please God, I shall go up to Church in the week, and go to receive my Communion on Sunday the same as usual, but I don't know how I shall feel not to see you there, nor Miss Dolling, nor nobody. You are gone, but you will never be forgotten by me. Give my love to Miss Dolling and Miss Blair and Geraldine and Miss Rowan, and if we do not meet in this world, I hope we shall in the next, where there won't be no sorrow.

"Yours affectionately."

The Bishop referred to is the Bishop of Winchester.

"Dear rev. farther, the new priest that come is so nice he do ofer up some beautful prayers and speaks so nice to us all but ther will never be on that will be nearest our hearts as you dear farther. O I bless the day I ented St. Agathas that wer I was first converted and O how your prayers have reached my heart I have cried may a time over them I have blessed you and I praye for you and your dear sisters for they was always good and kind to me a unworthy sinner but my dear Jesus will bless you all for what you have done for me for he knowed I was one of his lost sheep that was lost. O my dear Jesus good to me a sinner to take me back to his foild. I often think of the text the Bishop gave us. Yea I have loved thee with an everlasting love therefore with loveing kindness have I drawn thee and it is quite true for my dear Jesus how gently have he drawn me when I have been in any trouble I have heard words in my ear ask the Savour to healp you and he will carry you though, I never mean to neglect my dear Savour any more I will allways bless him not only with my lips but with all my live. so no more till I have the pleasure of writing to you again. from your most humble servant."

The Bishop referred to is the Bishop of Guildford, who confirmed her.

"DEAR FATHER
"According to your request I am sending a few words, they will be but few. I have not been to Church since Thursday Evening until the

11 celebration this morning. It will, I know, greatly please you to hear that the Church was quite full, mostly our own people, and it was a very nice service, 'Alike, but, oh, how different.' How my heart ached to see another priest in your place, my heart and eyes were full, but I remembered that we had to trust, wait patiently for the answer to the loving prayer that was going up to God from every heart of your people, and, oh, we do hope and pray that the time will soon come when we shall have you all back again with us. We cannot let you stay away from St. Agatha's. Our best love and respects to you and all the dear ladies. Trusting, dear Father, you will remember us in all your prayers, I remain in all truth and loyalty,

"Your deeply grieving child in God."

"DEAR MR. DOLLING,

"It seems like a dream to-day, more than ever, to be at St. Agatha's, without our good Father Dolling and other dear faces, yet the fact remains but too true, and yet not without you in the truest sense, for we met together in the Spirit this morning in the blessed Sacrament, and may our united prayers ascend to Almighty God to support you and yours and the whole of St. Agatha's in this our fiery trial and affliction, and that we may come forth purged and glorified, and win the victory by His dear mercy. Hoping yours and dear one's health may be good, even after the difficult task of leave taking. We have already made the acquaintance of Mr. Bull, he is a very nice man indeed, he preached a very appropriate sermon this morning from 1 Cor. iii. 13. I think we had a good number of communicants this morning at 7 o'clock, we were about 20 or 30, and, I believe, many more at 8. This evening, instead of the Mission Service, all the communicants who can will meet Mr. Bull in Church for further acquaintance. Now, with earnest hope of seeing you back at Portsmouth again very soon in good health, and with prayers for your own and dear St. Agatha's welfare,

"Believe me yours very sincerely."

"DEAR MR. DOLLING,

"It is not an easy thing to be off with the old love before you are on with the new. The new clergy are here, and they appear to be very earnest priests. Of course, one cannot judge how things will go along yet, but I hope for the best. God never has deserted St. Agatha's, and never will. Knowing you will have a great number of letters to read, I will not bore you with a long one.

"Yours very truly."

There was hardly a word of complaint out of four hundred letters, because they knew it would vex me; but everyone testified to the heartiness and affection with which they had met the tact and kindness and sympathy of Fr. Bull. Perhaps I ought not to write all this, but I feel so proud of them, so thankful to God for them. You will forgive me inserting a letter which Fr. Bull wrote me after he left.

"RADLEY VICARAGE, ABINGDON.
"DEAR FATHER DOLLING,
"I cannot leave the work at S. Agatha's without writing to tell you how deeply impressed I am by all that I have seen during my six weeks' charge. I came to the work with many misgivings, expecting to find your people made sore and irritable by all the troubles which brought your ministry at S. Agatha's to a close. But nothing could have been more beautiful than the patience with which they bore their sorrow, and the loyalty and courage with which they carried on the work of the parish.

"The points which made the profoundest impression on me were, I think, these:

"1. First, the true depth and reality of their love for our dear Redeemer. I dare not try to describe the manifestation of so sacred a feeling, but it is enough to say - that it made itself felt in every detail of work and worship, sanctifying what is sometimes looked upon as secular, inspiring every movement of ritual, and filling the outward forms of religion with a real outpouring of the heart.

"2. Then the very healthy type of devotion. It was 'Jesus only' in every variety of service; no wandering from the narrow way of true devotion into the sentimental bye-paths of 'fancy' religion.

"3. Real faith in the power of prayer. People at S. Agatha's had thoroughly realised that prayer has a great influence on the course of events, and they prayed with a readiness and fervour unknown in those places where the spirit of prayer has been strangled by the exclusive use of unvarying forms. I am sure that your people learned to pray so well, chiefly in the training of those services supplementary to matins and evensong.

"4. The combination of discipline and independence. This was most striking. Men of strong will and very decided character worked together in perfect harmony, and carried on the work of the parish with strength and vigour, because they recognised the difference between liberty and licence and the duty of loyalty. I found the parish practically self-working.

"5. The happy relationship between priest and people. The people look on their priest as a father and a friend, and not merely as a relieving officer to the parish. The account of your life and work among them, which, I believe, you are preparing, will explain how this was accomplished. But it will be a joy to you to know that the lessons you taught are not forgotten, and that your people readily extend the same confidence and love to any priest who brings them the same faith and sacraments. This is only one of many signs which show that you won these souls to Christ, and not merely to yourself.

"6. I cannot conclude without bearing witness to a fact which forces itself constantly on the attention of anyone who has seen the inside of your work; namely, that your faithful teaching of the doctrine of the Church about the future life, and our duty to those who have been taken from us for a time, is undoubtedly the secret of your work at S. Agatha's. To quote only one of many pathetic letters I received, one man writes thus: 'Prayers for and with our dear ones in paradise is the only thing that has made life tolerable to me for the last twenty-six years.' I felt all the time that I only saw a part of that dear family which you have gathered together round their Father's table, and that by far the larger part of those who shared in our prayers and Sacrifice were wanderers over sea and land in foreign countries, or souls at rest in paradise.

"Forgive me if anything I have said may seem to be patronising. You know my only wish is to bear witness to the depth and soundness of your work, which has been so much misunderstood and misrepresented. I will not dwell on the kind way in which you did your best to make my work easy for me, nor on the wonderful love

and patience with which your people welcomed me; it was as
overwhelming as it was undeserved.

"I am, yours very faithfully,

"Paul B. Bull."

Many younger clergy and people from a distance wounded by the
Bishop's action in insisting on a change in our services which had
been in use for eight years, wrote to me about going to Rome, but no
such word was even whispered in S. Agatha's. And this was not to be
wondered at; for neither from me, nor from my curates, nor from my
helpers, had they ever learned anything distinctly Roman, unless
reservation of the Blessed Sacrament can be so called. We tried to
make our religion manly, natural, dignified, and yet, in the truest
sense, homely. Every word from the altar was spoken plainly, so that
everyone could hear it. There were no concealments from the Bishop
or anyone else. If there had been, I should be there still.

Our one object was to translate into the new church all that there
had been in the old. My first idea of the new church was that it
should be built as plainly as possible. I, who had suffered so much
from begging, deemed it wrong to add any further burden to myself.
Besides, I felt I had already over-exhausted the generosity of my
many friends. But then, God sent Mr. Ball, the architect; and directly
I talked to him I saw how wrong this intention had been. If there is
one place which needs a magnificent and impressive church, it is a
slum. He had made a study of the church architecture which I liked
best, and which I had learned to know in Northern Italy. Directly you
enter the new S. Agatha's you realise it is a temple of God - of God
Eternal, of God Almighty; and, as it stands now, it has satisfied all my
desires. Every act done at the altar can be seen through the whole
church; every word spoken there, or from the pulpit, can be heard.
There is no use my trying to describe it; I do not think even Mr.
Ruskin ever made us understand what a building is like. I think one
of the reasons why the people at once felt at home in it was because
they had been working for it so long. For two years Miss Wright had
been directing a number of ladies in getting the vestments complete.
It is almost impossible for me to say what S. Agatha's owes to Miss
Wright. Then the people themselves had bought a, chalice and paten,

a set of Stations which cost £140, all of the cassocks; indeed, they had contributed over £330, all collected in small sums during the last three years. Winchester had done some special work for us, too. A little boy in Mr. Smith's house, who died some years ago, gave us our oak lectern, which cost £75. College, past and present, clothed with alabaster one of the pillars of the sanctuary. Three houses gave me nearly £60 for the oak panelling, on which the names from the old church are translated into the new. The great central pillar was clothed in alabaster and marble, and its capital carved in memory of one of my dear lads - a middy - who died of scarlet fever on board ship, and who had made his first Communion in old S. Agatha's. One of the granite pillars was paid for, and its capital carved in memory of a brother and sister very dear to me, who died within a year of one another. There is still a debt of £230 on the ornamentation of the church, part of it due to Messrs. Powell, who did the beautiful mosaic work in the Lady apse, and whom I am most anxious to pay off. It is wonderful how the magnificence of this mosaic work harmonises with the simplicity and beauty of Mr. Summer's sgraffitto work. It was a great gift of God to discover an artist who does not only superintend, but actually, with his own hands, religiously perfects his work. I felt, as I took my last look at the church, that it was impossible for me to express in words what I felt I owe, and what Landport and Winchester people owe, to Mr. Ball and Mr. Light - a debt which we can never repay. But there is a debt which we can pay - £100 to Mr. Ball, £1400 to Mr. Light, and £350 to the Bank, which they have advanced to me on Mr. Light's account.

My own pressing need of discharging these debts, perhaps, has made me forget one special benefit of a church like ours. It practically admits of continuous ornamentation. We have built but the roughest of brick walls. And I feel that this is of infinite importance, that each generation should be able to say, "my" church. That hideous desire to get things finished is the secret of the shoddy, ugly churches which disfigure Christianity, and having to pay nothing for them is one of the greatest wrongs that can be done to a congregation. These great wall-spaces of Italian architecture are designed for the very purpose of being the ignorant man's Bible, and the poor man's opportunity of offering his mite to God; and I have no doubt that S. Agatha's people

NEW SAINT AGATHA'S

will, by degrees, create it, what Mr. Ruskin says S. Mark's is to the Venetians - "an open Bible," which even the most unlearned and ignorant may easily read.

XVI.
A Plea For Toleration.

MY work in Landport is finished. I hand over to the Bishop of Winchester all necessary plant for the future of S. Agatha's - Church, Schools, Mission House, Parsonage, Gymnasium, Clubs, Almshouses - which the generosity of Wykehamists and my own friends has enabled me to build for the Church of England. I hand him over a parish with a communicants' roll of 441, so united that for ten years there has never been a difference amongst us, so full of zeal for Holy Religion that they have created admiration and wonder in the heart of that most experienced missioner Father Maturin, and who welcomed, without one single murmur, Father Bull, who took my place, when the Bishop's demand for alteration in the services caused me to resign. Into the Bishop's hands, and the hands of my successor appointed by Winchester College, I place this great trust to which God appointed me ten and a half years ago, and I pray God that they may be able to administer it with greater zeal, self-denial, and success than I have been able.

I have taken it for granted that this book will generally be read by those who know S. Agatha's, and therefore I have frequently spoken about persons and things without any introduction, knowing that these readers would know what I meant; but for the sake of others who do not know me or the work, I should like to make a few explanations. In the first place "I" always stands for "we," and "my" always stands for "ours"; for I have had round me a body of the most devoted helpers that parish priest ever had, not only my own sisters and the ladies who lived with them, my fellow-clergy, and the laymen who lived with me, but the day-school and Sunday-school teachers, the district visitors, all who served in the church, either on the altar or in the choir, my own personal clerks, the servants in my own and

Miss Boiling's house, our shopwoman, and many more too-numerous to mention. Every parochial plan was well discussed by those who had to administer it; objections were stated, differences were heard, but when once we had arrived at what was deemed to be the right course, one mouth spoke the judgment - one brain, one hand, executed it. There was no degradation of service, there was no unstinted labour, there was no demand on heart and enthusiasm that I have ever asked and been refused by one of my workers. I could almost dare to use some of S. Paul's expressions with regard to the unselfish loyalty with which I have been supported; and I know the parish felt that, whether it was they or I; so we preached, and so they believed. Might I give two instances?

As I have said before, I am an unlearned man, unable to pass even my "little go" at Cambridge. When Charles Osborne came to me, I had no knowledge of exact theology at all, except what I had been able to scrape together during one year at Salisbury Theological College, where the Rev. E. B. Ottley was particularly kind and patient with me. But Osborne devoted an hour a day all the time he was with me to talking theology with me. There is no method of learning so easy as the conversational method, especially such conversation as his, and when the opportunity came to me to occupy London pulpits, he prepared the notes of many of my sermons, and looked up the references; and ever since he left me, though he now has work almost as time-exhausting as my own, he has never failed to send me at Lent, and at other times when I needed them, courses of sermons. I have often felt little better than a humbug, delivering sermons which are the fruit of his brain. And when I left Portsmouth, my then secretary followed me to London, and has remained with me, so as to prevent the compositors who set up this book committing suicide, or the world being scandalised with my bad spelling. These are but two little instances of countless acts of love and devotion which it has been our extraordinary privilege for the last ten years to enjoy; and when you hear of trades' unions of curates and vicars, and of disloyalty on the one side, and humiliations on the other, I should like you to realise that our work was successful because, though I was the apparent doer of it, I merely represented a community bound together by the tenderest ties of mutual service. People take a very exaggerated view of mission work. It is not only the pleasantest and most rewarding, but it is really the easiest done. Preaching about a great deal, and giving retreats and missions, enables one to judge, I think, pretty fairly of the difficulties of other clergymen's work, and I am quite sure that I am speaking only the literal truth when I say that I have never been in any parish where the work was as easy as in my own. Of course, we added to ourselves many things that were not strictly parochial; and if these had not been begun, and we had merely stuck to working amongst our own people, this truth would have been even more apparent. Faith in humanity is the foundation of all mission work, very easy to be attained in a slum where, every single day, some soul reveals to you progress; very difficult to attain in a parish where your church is well filled by a respectable congregation. Then a greater elasticity of method is allowed, and it was just the attempt to check this that never could have occurred if Bishop Thorold had lived. And yet I think that if reasonable people, unprejudiced and unbiassed, would consider the Prayer Book, and the methods by which it has been interpreted for the last fifty years, they would be less anxious to desire to curtail this greater liberty of method.

At best surely the Prayer Book is a compromise, for which, indeed, we may be most grateful to Almighty God, when we consider the character of those who constructed it, and the Court pressure under which many of them were continually coerced. But surely a compromise, fond as we are of them in England, is never a lasting arrangement. Fifty years ago people might conscientiously call our Liturgy incomparable, because, as a witty Irishman said, they had no others to compare it with. But now, when the inexhaustible treasures of both East and West have been rediscovered by us, and when those Catholic doctrines, long hidden away in the hearts of a few learned clerics, were, by the Oxford movement, scattered broadcast over England, the method by which those doctrines alone could be understanded of the people, was by interpreting the Prayer Book according to Catholic ceremonial, and the progress which has been made in this interpretation is a fact that we, who see its effects, can hardly appreciate. Is it not true to say that fifty years ago almost every single Bishop on the English bench would have proclaimed the priest a traitor, and endeavoured to deprive him, for doctrines that are taught, and for ceremonies which are performed, in twenty-five per cent, of the churches in their dioceses to-day? Remember, the things which have been condemned in S. Agatha's are done in a large number of churches in England. Earnest souls everywhere are crying out for Masses to be said for their dear dead. There is no service in the Prayer Book appointed for this purpose. But the Catholic priest who understands and appreciates the piety of this desire, who believes himself that he has this treasure committed to him by God, will not surely be deemed disloyal to the Church of England if he ventures to use either the service in the Prayer Book of Edward VI., which our own Prayer Book declares "doth not contain anything contrary to the Word of God, or to sound doctrine," or chooses from some ancient source a like office. It seems to me that this is a far more honest practice than to use in a forced sense the Commendatory Prayer from the Visitation of the Sick, the first prayer in the Burial Service, or the first Good Friday collect, the use which my successor has adopted in deference, I suppose, to the Bishop's wish. I know his great integrity of purpose, and his utter honesty of mind, and, therefore, I am sure that he considers his method a more honest one than mine. But the chief thing which commended S. Agatha's to Bishop Thorold, to my numerous supporters, and to my poor people, was the plainness of speech and calling things by their names, which oftentimes superficial gazers may deem unwise, but which I have ever found to pay in the long run. But if it might be said that putting in a new prayer is disloyal, no one can say that leaving out a prayer, or disregarding a rubric is disloyal. I do not suppose that there is any church in England where every prayer is said, and every rubric obeyed; nay, the service would be intolerable, impossible, if it were so. People have, however, a convenient way of saying, "This rubric is obsolete; that prayer may be lawfully left out, that exhortation never read." Who is the best judge of that? The parish priest who has laboured ten years amongst his people, and knows every one of them, and the Bishop who has visited, loved, and blessed that work for four years, or the Bishop who has been in the diocese for three weeks? Two rubrics stand side by side in the Book of Common Prayer. One of them as to having notice given of

Communion I obeyed, the other as to the number of communicants I disobeyed. Ninety-nine clergy out of a hundred disobey the one I obeyed, eighty obey the one that I disobeyed. Let me illustrate, by my successor's action, the enormous difficulty of obeying both. He says, You must give notice if you are coming to the Holy Communion, and he has told the people that, unless notice is given so that he may know that there will be communicants, the Children's Mass at 10, and the High Mass at 11, must be given up. The notice is to be given in on Saturday night. If two communicants give notice, or one, or none, what would his action be? Would he wait till people came to church and tell them that there would be a different kind of service, and thus prevent many of his faithful from being present at a Celebration, which many of them believe to be a Christian obligation, or would he get certain people to promise, three for 10, and three for 11 each Sunday? - a strain on their loyalty that I, whom they loved and knew, would never have dared to demand, for the working woman with children an utter impossibility, for the District Visitor from Southsea a walk of a mile and a half there and back, entailing most likely an illness and a breakdown, for the working man living with all his children round him, breakfast a common meal shared by all on Sunday - I am not talking of the irreligious man who eats his breakfast, and lies in bed till one or two p.m. - the binding upon him of a burden, which we ourselves, who are often forced to say late Masses, can hardly sustain. This line of thought applies just as well to the daily Masses in a place in which it was utterly impossible, with all my workers round me, to manufacture six communicants every day. I have ventured to go into this question again at length, because I am anxious that the public should understand it. If the Bishops are going to make an attack all round on beneficed as well as unbeneficed clergy, on High, Low, and Broad equally, then I and my people would have no right to complain. But I doubt very much whether the Church of England could stand the strain of such an attack. If such an attack is to be made it must be uniform, and not according to the individual mind of the Bishop; Bishop Perowne might succeed Bishop King, Bishop Eyle might succeed Bishop Temple. And surely this danger ought to be realised before fresh power is put into the Bishops' hands, such power as is proposed in the recent Patronage

Act, which would have meant in my case that if I had been presented to a living, either in the diocese of Durham or of Worcester, I should not only have been refused by the Bishop, but - as I read the Act - my patron would have lost his nomination, and the prelate would have appointed his own nominee. Far more dangerous would it be, as a recent bill in Convocation proposed, to allow the Bishop to be sole judge of what rubrics are obsolete, and what must of necessity be observed.

"We are told that these are days when every Church Society is being starved, when the Bishops can neither get money nor men for their great overgrown dioceses, and therefore that the masses are in a large extent lost to the Church of England. Here is a place where over £50,000 has been spent in ten years, only £760 of it coming from a Diocesan Fund. Here is a place where three clergy, and many earnest laymen and women, have been working at no cost to the official resources of the Church at all. Here is a place where large numbers of the poorest and most ignorant have been instructed in the saving truths of Holy Religion. Here is a place which the late Bishop of the diocese fostered with truest tenderness and care. I do not venture to ask the question which I was going to ask, but I leave it to the judgment of my readers to answer the question themselves. I know that one answer is conceivable. "No work, no labour, no success is any excuse, when disobedience to the Prayer Book is practised alongside of it." But does anyone pretend to believe that this is the consistent method of the Church of England; or, if it had been so for the last fifty years, would one spark of life have been left in her?

If this little book has interested you at all, I would earnestly ask you to help me to pay off my debt. During the last three months people have been very generous to me, and I have paid off £800. This leaves me still owing £2290. Many Winchester men are very anxious, I know, that the Wykehamist Committee should become responsible for this debt, and I shall be very grateful if they do, because that might enable me to raise from the bank the money that I require to pay the builders. But even if they make themselves responsible, I feel it to be my bounden duty to do all I can to get this money together, for all the time that they are collecting it, they will be able to give my successor very little for his Mission work. I know that in many things he excels me, but I know that I am a better beggar than he is. He will require every penny that he can possibly scrape together, and so I am most anxious to set all Wykehamical resources free, by paying off this sum as quickly as possible.

Many people write and ask me, What are you going to do yourself? The answer to that rests in other hands than mine. When this debt is paid, if the Church of England offers me work, and I believe that it is God's intention that I should accept it, I will at once. In the meantime I am trying to learn a little lesson that one of my dearest children, a Jesuit priest, wrote down for me, "God allows you to build the fibre of your brain, the blood of your heart, into a temple for His glory, and then with one breath of His nostril o'erturns it, that He may see whether you will bear this also."

APPENDIX

"17, CLARENCE STREET, LANDPORT,
"September 28th, 1895.

"MY LORD BISHOP,

"We are taking possession of our new church on October 27th. It practically is joined by the vestries to the old church, which was licensed for celebrations by Bishop Harold Browne, and your predecessor did not think it would require a new licence.

"As at present the district is not a legal Parish, the question of consecration does not arise.

"I am, your lordship's obedient servant,

"R. Radclyffe Dolling."

"DALMENY PARK, EDINBURGH,
"4th October, 1895.

"DEAR MR. DOLLING,

"Your letter of Sept. 28th has only now reached me in Scotland. Everything has been upset somewhat during our removal from one house to another.

"I am greatly interested to learn that you hope to enter so soon upon the use of the new church. I shall be anxious, so far as possible, to meet your wishes in every way with regard to licence. If you were told by Bishop Thorold that no fresh licence would be necessary, I have no doubt such is the case, but I should, myself, have thought it would probably be better that a new licence should be given for the new building. This, however, we can talk over when we meet, and I trust the meeting may take place ere long, as I am most anxious to see something of your work, upon the spot. I have heard much of it, and I pray God to grant you all guidance and blessing among the difficulties by which you are surrounded.

"Bishop Thorold's opinion that no fresh licence is required will, at least, justify you in going forward now with all your arrangements, and if it turns out hereafter that it is desirable to issue a fresh licence, there will, I imagine, be no difficulty in doing so. I hope to be at Farnham next week, and to enter as speedily as possible upon diocesan work. I know I may rely upon your giving me the help of your prayers.

"I am, yours very truly,
"RANDALL WINTON."

"17, CLARENCE STREET, LANDPORT,
"October 7th, 1895.
"MY DEAR LORD BISHOP,

"I am most grateful for your kind letter. Bishop Thorold's idea was that until the church was consecrated (that would be as soon as the parish was created), the old licence would suffice. But I quite feel that your lordship's wish is most reasonable, and as soon as convenient to yourself the required formalities could be performed.

"We have never ceased to pray for your lordship since your election, and there are no priest or people more desirous to welcome you.

"The Bishop of Southwell, or the Bishop of Reading, will be with us at the opening, or during the octave. There is one of my soldier children on furlough, who needs to be confirmed. Might he have your permission to do it?

"Yours very obediently,
"R. R. DOLLING."

"FARNHAM CASTLE, SURREY,
"10th October, 1895.
"DEAR MR, DOLLING,

"I thank you for your letter. I will consider the question of licence. In the meantime, do not let the postponement of a decision on that point interfere in any way with your plans and arrangements.

"With regard to the confirmation of the lad you refer to, I should be quite willing that the Bishop of Southwell or the Bishop of Reading should confirm him if you think this desirable, and if such

Bishop is willing, at your request, to do it.
"I am, yours very truly,
"RANDALL WINTON."

"FARNHAM,
"17th October, 1895.
"DEAR MR. DOLLING,
"I have considered the question of a licence for your new church,
or rather, for you to minister therein, and it seems clear that such a
licence ought to be issued. I have, therefore, asked the Rural Dean, in
ordinary course, to send me the usual report that he has visited the
building, and that all is in due order.

"Of course, in strict accordance with rule, no service should take
place in the building till the proper licence (after the Rural Dean's
letter) has been received by you.

"But as I know you have been making arrangements for your
opening services, and that it was owing to the change of Bishops that
you did not sooner apply to me, I am quite willing that your
arrangements should be proceeded with, and you will, of course,
understand that, in the very improbable event of any question arising
as to the building or its due 'appointments,' I am not to be regarded
as hereby prejudging such question.

"I am sure it will be your wish that all should be in due order, and
I pray that the blessing of God may rest in rich measure on you and
on your work.
"I am, yours very truly,
"RANDALL WINTON."

"WINCHESTER COLLEGE MISSION, LANDPORT,
"October 18th, 1895.
"MY DEAR LORD BISHOP,
"I shall be very glad to see Canon Jacob. I am very distressed to
hear from . . . that you are hurt at my action about the Opening, and I
venture to assure you that the arrangements that I have made are
those which I contemplated before there was any vacancy in the See,
arrangements which I had planned in accordance with the action of
the two late Bishops towards the Mission.

"Bishop Harold Browne would never come here at all, or send his Suffragan, but allowed me to choose a Bishop to confer Confirmation.

"Bishop Thorold came himself, and sent his Suffragan, to Confirm, but otherwise he never took part in any ceremony in the church, and he personally often told me that he greatly disliked the ritual. And even when he came to Confirm, as of course the service was altogether his own and not ours, he did not allow the acolytes to wear red cassocks, and when I pointed out that the Crucifix was carried in front of the Procession, he ordered it not to be used, though when I told him there was another on the altar, and offered to take it down, he said, 'No; I shall not see that one.' I should certainly never have asked him to come to any other service at S. Agatha's, as I am sure it would have pained him very deeply, and my people here are so very ignorant, that I could not have altered it, had he happened to be present.

"I would not have you think from this, that I did not revere and respect him, even perhaps love him, and we have oftentimes been very near to each other in prayer. And, therefore, I had determined not to ask him to take any part in the ceremonies connected with the Opening of the church, until the time of the Consecration should come, and for the same reason, of course, I would not ask his Suffragan, though the Bishop of Southampton is a Wykehamist, and I should much like to have had him here.

"I do not like to intrude upon your Lordship at such great length, but I should not like your Lordship to think that I am at all lacking in respect to your person or to your great office.

Yours very obediently',

"R. R. DOLLING."

"FARNHAM CASTLE, SURREY,
20th October 1895.

"DEAR MR. DOLLING,

"I thank you for your letter, but either you must, I think, have misunderstood ... or he must have misunderstood me. Perhaps both.

"I perfectly understand the position as you now explain it, namely, that you are simply following out arrangements which were made in Bishop Thorold's time, and which were such as you thought he would desire.

"Nothing could be further from my mind than to be 'hurt' by anything that has passed. I have too much respect for you and for your work. I feel sure you have wished to do all that is right, and (as I said in a former letter) I am anxious not to disturb arrangements which were made before I was responsible.

"I hear to-day from the Rural Dean that he has arranged with you to pay his visit next Wednesday, so perhaps after all the new licence may reach you in time.

"I pray that the blessing and guidance of God may be given you in your difficult task.

"I am, yours very truly,

"RANDALL WINTON,"

"FARNHAM CASTLE, SURREY,
24th October 1895

"DEAR MR. DOLLING,

"I have this morning received the Rural Dean's report of his visit yesterday to your new church.

"While expressing his admiration of the building, he tells me the fittings are not yet *in situ*, though they will for the most part be ready by Saturday next. He cannot therefore report upon them in detail. But speaking generally, it is clear that the arrangements are in so forward a condition that, if no question of difficulty arose, a licence might be sent to you forthwith, authorising you in the usual form to minister the offices of the Church therein. Of course, if it were a question of now consecrating the church, and thereby giving legal authority to what stands therein, I should require, as always, a more detailed report when everything is *in situ*. But as you do not ask for Consecration at present, legal questions in the technical sense do not arise in quite the same manner.

"There is, however, one important matter mentioned by the Rural Dean which I must at once bring before you. Canon Jacob says: 'It is proposed to place a third altar in the middle of the South Aisle . . . and the altar is avowedly to be used for Masses for the Dead. Mr. Dolling said that Bishop Thorold saw this in the temporary church (there it was simply the second altar, corresponding to that in the east end of the south aisle of the new church), and intensely disliked it. Here, however, it assumes a far greater prominence, for it is not the altar for ordinary daily use, as in the temporary church, but simply to be used for Masses for the Dead. Mr. Dolling lays the greatest stress on this.'

"Now here is a matter of supreme importance. I have no wish to prejudge any legal question which may arise, and I am not aware whether any authoritative decision has been given in the Church Courts respecting the legality of a third altar in such a position in such a church.

"But I should obviously be treating you unfairly, were I now to send you a licence virtually sanctioning such an arrangement as this, and then, hereafter, when the time comes for consecrating the church, and when your people have grown used to the arrangement, to direct the removal of so prominent a feature on the ground that when duly submitted for the consideration of the Diocesan Court, it is found to be illegal. My belief is that, if the circumstances are such as Canon Jacob has described, it would be so declared, though in this I may, of course, be mistaken.

"I do not know what sanction was originally obtained for the plans of your church. If plans distinctly exhibiting this feature received Bishop Thorold's signature and sanction, I would ask you to tell me so at once. In lack, however, of such information, I must ask that the church be not publicly opened for Divine Service until a question so important as this has been submitted to the proper authorities for decision, or until the altar in question has been removed from the building. I think you must see that this is no matter of subordinate detail. Were it such, I should not wish, in the very peculiar circumstances of this case, to be over-particular at this moment. But large principles are involved, and it would therefore be quite wrong to prejudge what may be the ultimate decision on so important a matter, by formally licensing you to minister in a building containing thus prominently a feature upon which, if the Rural Dean correctly reports, you lay the greatest stress.

"I am exceedingly sorry to seem thus to interfere at the last moment with the arrangements you have made; but you are aware that this is not my fault, and I think I am only treating you with such fairness and openness as I should wish myself to meet with in like circumstances. Let me recall to you briefly what has passed.

"On October 2nd I received from you a letter telling me, for the first time, that you proposed taking possession of the new church on October 27th, and adding that Bishop Thorold did not think it would require a new licence. In my reply, while I sanctioned your going forward with the arrangements which had been already made for the opening services, I said that I should myself have thought it would probably be better that a new licence should be given for the new building. To this you quite assented, and I accordingly directed the Rural Dean to pay the usual preliminary visit. The first intimation I received from you that any difficult question would be likely to arise was in your letter of October 18th, in which you said: 'I should certainly never have asked Bishop Thorold to come to any other service at St. Agatha's (i.e., other than Confirmation), as I am sure it would have pained him very deeply.' I merely recall these facts in order to remind you that I could not have written sooner on this subject. Had I had reason to suppose at an earlier date that there were likely to be difficulties of this kind, I should have asked you to postpone the opening services until the question of licence had been further considered.

"You are aware from my former letters how cordially I appreciate and value your vigorous work at Landport, and how anxious I am to promote and help it in every legitimate way. I am most anxious not to make a fuss about trifles, and I desire to recognise to the full the due elasticity and variety desirable in the services of the Church, especially in such neighbourhoods as yours. You will never find me inclined to be needlessly rigid about comparative trifles, but a Bishop's responsibility is so grave that when large questions arise he must of necessity act with the utmost care.

"I trust that it may be possible for you so to modify the arrangements as to enable your proposed opening services to take place, postponing for the present the decision upon the particular point to which I have called attention.

"If you desire to see me upon the subject, I shall be at your service here at any hour to-morrow, except 1.30 to 3, when I have

another engagement. If you are coming, please telegraph to say so.
I am, yours very truly,
"RANDALL WINTON."

"Since writing the above I have thought it may be a convenience to you that I should send it to you by hand. My chaplain accordingly bears it."

An interview took place on October 25th. (See p. 141.)

(See p. 141.)

"FARNHAM CASTLE, SURREY,
"25th October, 1895.

"DEAR MR. DOLLING,

"I must send a few lines to thank you for the honest and simple straightforwardness and frankness with which you this morning put before me your position in the question which has arisen, and for your ultimate acquiescence in the suggestion I made as to your proper course of procedure.

"I pray God that to each of us, in our respective positions of anxious and responsible work, may be given from on high that right judgment in all things for which we are accustomed to ask; and whatever may ultimately be decided with respect to the particular point which is now under consideration, I feel sure we shall not lose or loose that bond of fellowship which unites in heart and spirit those who have in common the one great aim of advancing to the best of our power, and in accordance with what seems to us to be the due order of our Church of England, the Kingdom of our Blessed Lord.

"I am, with kindest regards,
"Very truly yours,
"RANDALL WINTON."

"WINCHESTER COLLEGE MISSION, LANDPORT,
"25th October 1895

"MY DEAR LORD BISHOP,

"I send you the statement I read out to my people. I have directed the architect to prepare you the plans. I shall be grateful if, when you receive them, you will give me a date when I may expect your decision.

"I am, yours very obediently,
"R. R. DOLLING."

"As our new church practically joins on to the old church, the late Bishop considered that no new licence would be needed. When I communicated this fact to our new Bishop, he desired that a new licence should be granted, and therefore sent the Rural Dean to report on the fabric and ornaments of the church.

"Acting on his report, the Bishop feels that it is impossible to grant this licence until he has consulted authorities as to the legality of the Third Altar, the one which you beautified in memory of Henry Ross, and which used to stand in the old church with the Memorials of the Dead around it. He therefore wrote to me that the licence would not be granted until the Altar was removed. My own feelings under these circumstances were that it would be better for us to remain in the old church, and not to open the new church. But when I saw the Bishop this morning, he very much disliked this idea, and suggested, as an alternative, that we should proceed with the opening, screening off the Altar and the Memorials of the Dead; that the plans should be at once submitted to him, showing every detail; and that he should proceed after due time to deliver judgment; if he can license the Altar, I am to remove the screen; if he cannot, I am at once to resign, so that a successor may be appointed who will remove the Altar and the Memorials."

"FARNHAM CASTLE, SURREY,
"26th October, 1895.
"DEAR MR. DOLLING,
"I have just received your letter enclosing a copy of the intimation you read yesterday to your people. I feel sure it was not your wish to say anything which would convey a mistaken impression of what has passed between us on the question at issue, but you have certainly done so, however unintentionally.

"Your words, 'The Bishop wrote to me that the Licence would not be granted until the Altar was removed,' are surely inconsistent with the purport of the actual letter, in which I tried to point out to you that the question was one which I ought not to prejudge, and that it required time for consideration.

"Again, I never, either in letter or conversation, desired you to screen off the 'Memorials of the Dead.' If the temporary screening off of the site intended for the proposed third altar necessarily involves this - which I did not understand - it is merely incidental, and your words would convey the wholly false impression that I had objected to the erection of 'Memorials of the Dead.' I have not seen them, and I do not know their precise character, nor did I mention them in any way.

"Most important of all, your final sentence practically says that in the event of such a third altar being found to be inadmissible, it is my wish that you should resign.

"You will remember that on the contrary I expressed my great regret at hearing from you that such would in that event be your course of action, although you assured me that in any circumstances you had already settled to leave S. Agatha's a few months hence. My own wish would be strongly against your resignation.

"I feel sure, as I have said, that it was not your intention to mislead any who may have heard or read your words, and I do not doubt that you will desire at once to set the matter right, by giving publicity to this letter or otherwise.

"I am, dear Mr. Dolling,

"Yours very truly,

"RANDALL WINTON."

"WINCHESTER COLLEGE MISSION, LANDPORT,

"October 28th, 1895.

"MY DEAR LORD BISHOP,

"I am very sorry, indeed, if I have in any way misrepresented our conversation, but in your letter to me of the 24th, you say:

"'I must ask that the church be not publicly opened for Divine Service, until a question so important as this has been submitted to the proper authorities for decision, or until the altar in question has been removed from the building.'

"You yourself told me, when I saw you, that it would be a scandal if the church was not opened, and, therefore, surely it was only left to me by your letter of the 24th, to create a scandal or to remove the altar.

"Secondly, the memorials are practically a part of the altar, as a frame is to the picture, and without these memorials, the altar would, I take it, be unobjectionable, or rather, as I think you said yourself, the question is not the red-tape question whether there is to be a third altar, but whether it is to be an altar of this kind - *i.e.*, Dedicated to the Dead. There will be the twelve Celebrations said at it every week, and only two of them will be said for the Dead. I certainly supposed that your injunction, therefore, referred to the character of the thing as a whole.

"Thirdly, I certainly do not say that you would wish me to resign. What I do say is, 'If he cannot license the altar, I am at once to resign, so that a successor may be appointed, who will remove the altar and the memorials.' This surely does not convey the meaning that you wish me to resign, but that the action which you quite conscientiously may be compelled to take, may necessitate my resignation, which is quite a different thing. I believe that there is not a man in all the Diocese more anxious that I should remain than you are. I have written to the Portsmouth paper which mentioned the fact. I enclose you the letter.

"Canon Jacob's letter which I enclose, and which please return, may enable the question to be decided in a more satisfactory way than by your Lordship's personal judgment.

"I hope that in a few weeks the fabric of the church will be free of debt. I have built a Parsonage House, and I have £1100 in hand towards the endowment. If on these terms the district can be created into a parish, the question would then be one which could be decided by the highest ecclesiastical legal authorities.

"I should be very grateful for your Lordship's opinion on this matter.

"Ever your obedient servant,
"R. R. DOLLING."

"FARNHAM CASTLE, SURREY,
"29th October, 1895.
"DEAR MR. DOLLING,
" I thank you for your letter of yesterday. If, as I suppose, the

letter to the *Evening News* which you send me in manuscript has been published in that paper, it meets the chief objection I felt to the wording of the memorandum you sent me, and I am obliged to you for making the point clear to those who might have misunderstood it. If you are satisfied, I do not wish to dwell further upon the other points mentioned in my letter to you, although I still think your words would convey to most hearers or readers a different impression from that which you can yourself have intended. With regard to the suggestion, that an endeavour should now be made to have the district legally assigned, and the church duly consecrated as a parish church, I should like a little time for consideration and consultation with others before giving you definite advice. You will remember that the Diocese is still new to me, and that in a matter like this local knowledge is almost essential to a right decision. Such knowledge I will do my best to acquire speedily. I retain in the meantime Canon Jacob's letter upon the subject. I am, yours very truly,

"RANDALL WINTON."

"S. AGATHA, LANDPORT,
"November 4th, 1895.

"MY DEAR LORD BISHOP,

"I send you plans of east end, with its two apses and altars, and north and south side of church, showing stations and third altar. The only place not shown is the baptistery under the tower. I had intended putting an altar in this for the use of parents on the morning of the baptism of their children. I did not speak of this to Bishop Thorold, for it was only suggested to me when I showed the baptistery and font to some of the mothers, and they said what a comfort and help it would be to take Communion in the baptistery. I will send you a little plan of this. I mentioned it to Canon Jacob, but he said there was no use in speaking of it to you. Most of the columns, paintings, &c., are memorials; they will all have on them, 'Pray for the soul of,' etc. The altars all have candlesticks on them. There is a large crucifix by the pulpit.

"Ever yours very truly,
"R. R. DOLLING."

We always have confession in public in church, so there would be three seats for this purpose in the church.

FARNHAM CASTLE, SURREY,

6th November 1895

"DEAR MR. DOLLING,"

"I received last night your letter of the previous day, enclosing the plans. Now that I have these before me I can better consider the subject, and ask such counsel as seems desirable. It is difficult for me to say by what day I may be able to give you my decision upon the matter.

"I am much pressed at present with work of every kind, but I will take care that there is no unnecessary delay. I should hope, in a fortnight's time at the latest, to be able to write to you definitely.

"It is possible I may wish to see you again. May I ask you to tell me whether any particular day in the week would be specially convenient or inconvenient to you for the journey to Farnham?

"Nothing could, I think, be gained by my seeing the architect, as the plans seem perfectly clear.

"I am, yours very truly,

"RANDALL WINTON."

"FARNHAM CASTLE, SURREY,

"11th November, 1895.

"DEAR MR. DOLLING,

"Would it suit you to call here next Saturday morning, November 16th, or, if more convenient, to dine and sleep here on Friday night, the 15th, leaving as early as you like on Saturday morning?

"I am anxious, if possible, not to postpone our interview beyond next week. Please let me know when I may expect you.

"I am, yours very truly,

"RANDALL WINTON."

A prolonged interview took place on November 15th. (See p. 170.)

"CLARENCE STREET, LANDPORT,"

15th November, 1895.

"MY DEAR LORD BISHOP,

"I am very grateful to you for your patience this afternoon. You will be glad to hear that I do not feel any the worse. It would be a great relief to me if your lordship could tell me about the date when your lordship is likely to deliver judgment. Of course, we do not mean for one moment to hasten you, but our own minds would be more at rest if we knew about the date.

"Mr. Gresham desires to join with me in many thanks to Mrs. Davidson for her great kindness.

"Yours very obediently,

"R. R. Dolling."

"WINCHESTER COLLEGE MISSION, LANDPORT,"
16th November, 1895.

"MY DEAR LORD BISHOP,

"I send you our Vespers of the Blessed Sacrament, our Stations, our Mass for the Dead, and our children's Mass book, and the rules of our Communicants' Society. Our conversation of yesterday was so different from what I have had with Bishops in former days. They seemed to desire to deal with things concerning which complaint had been made to them, and so, when I had ventured on other details of our service here, they stopped me, as though to say, 'That question is not before me, I do not desire to know it.' It seemed to me, yesterday, that your attitude was the very opposite of this. You wanted to know everything we do at S. Agatha's, and, therefore, praying over it all last night, and thinking about it, I was very anxious to discover if I was perfectly honest and straightforward, and I think I was. But when I was leaving your room you said to me, 'Have you anything more to say?' I took that, at the moment, to mean, 'Is there any defence more that you would like to make concerning your doings?' But, on thinking it over, it seems to me it may have meant, 'Are there any other services or practices that you ought to tell me about?' If this is your meaning, pray let me know, and I will send to you, in detail, everything else that we do. If, on the other hand, this thought of mine is over scrupulosity, please don't answer this letter.

"Your obedient servant,

"R. R. DOLLING."

"FARNHAM CASTLE, SURREY,
"21st November, 1895.

"DEAR MR. DOLLING,

"I have not had a moment in which to reply to your letter received two days ago.

"When I asked you at our recent interview whether you had anything more to say, I did not in the least mean to ask you for a detailed account of all the services you hold. Some day I should be interested to hear from you about everything, in order that I may thoroughly understand your position and teaching. But all I desired in our recent interview was to understand the present situation in all its bearings, so that my decision may be based upon a really sufficient knowledge.

"I have been so much pressed during this last week by unexpected matters, including the illness and death of a dear friend, that I have been ceaselessly on the railway, and it has been impossible for me to give to S. Agatha's matters the attention they deserve. Hence there may be a little delay in my sending you the formal letter I have promised. I can only say that I am doing my best.

"I remain, yours very truly,

"RANDALL WINTON."

"FARNHAM CASTLE, SURREY,
"7th December, 1895.

"DEAR MR. DOLLING,

"I am now able to write to you definitely upon the question which has arisen with regard to S. Agatha's church, and as you may probably wish to make my letter public, it will be convenient that I should briefly recall what has taken place. On October 2nd, a few days after I had become Bishop of Winchester, I heard from you that you had made arrangements to open the new church for divine service on October 27th. With a view, therefore, to your receiving the necessary licence, I directed Canon Jacob, as Rural Dean, to pay the customary preliminary visit to the church, and to report to me whether all was in due order. On October 24th I received this report.

He told me of the beauty and dignity of the building, and its general suitableness for divine service in a great parish. The fittings and ornaments were not yet *in situ*, and he was, therefore, unable to report upon them in detail. But he directed my attention, as in duty bound, to the structural arrangements for Holy Communion. These, as shown in his report, and in his subsequent explanations to me with appended plans, are as follows: One large Holy Table or Altar in the usual position in the centre of the east end of the church; a second (for less largely attended services) at the east end of the south aisle; and a third in the south aisle, placed against the side wall of the church. It is also your wish to place a fourth in your Baptistery at the west end of the north aisle, but that question is not at present before us.

"When Canon Jacob paid his official visit to the church, the proposed third altar had not yet been erected; and after full correspondence and conversation between yourself and me upon the subject, it was decided that the opening services should be held in accordance with the arrangements you had already made before I became Bishop, but that the site of the proposed third altar should be temporarily curtained off, and its erection at the least postponed, so that I should have time before issuing formal licence for the conduct of divine service in the building, to consider the arrangements proposed. You urged me to give you an answer as speedily as possible, as in the event of my being unable to sanction the proposed arrangements you would feel it necessary to withdraw immediately from S. Agatha's, instead of remaining until Easter next, when you proposed in any case to resign.

"As it is not proposed that the church should be consecrated at present, the question raised does not, and, indeed, cannot, now come formally before the Diocesan Court. Pending consecration, it rests with the Bishop to grant or withhold at his discretion the necessary licence for the conduct of divine service in the new building. In order, therefore, to understand in all its bearings the question to which you attach so much importance, I have, in addition to our correspondence, had two prolonged interviews with you; and I am anxious again to express to you my appreciation of the honest and straightforward readiness you have throughout shown to give me all possible information as to your usages and the opinions on which they are based. In a matter of this kind, where we have but one object - namely, to arrive at a right conclusion in accordance with the doctrines and laws of the Church of England - it is of paramount importance that there should be no concealment or reserve in setting the facts before the Bishop, on whom lies the grave responsibility of decision.

"I am cordially grateful to you, therefore, for freeing me from any difficulty of that sort. After deliberately weighing all that you have put before me, I have come to the conclusion that I should act wrongly were I, on my personal authority, now to sanction the erection and use of the proposed third altar in the situation and for the purposes you have described to me. When the church is consecrated it would, of course, be possible for you, or your successor, to apply to the Diocesan Court for a faculty for the erection of such a third altar; and, were the faculty refused, you would have the opportunity - which you tell me you desire - of bringing the question before the higher Courts on appeal from the decision of the Chancellor.

"In the meantime, as I have fully explained to you in conversation, I cannot, in exercising my discretion upon a proposition so unusual, regard the question as merely the technical one - may there be three altars or holy tables in one church?

"It is easy to conceive a church or cathedral of such dimensions or construction as to render it desirable to extend yet further the principle upon which a second altar or holy table has been sanctioned in many of our churches for more convenient use when the number of communicants is small and, whatever might be the legal decision on such a point, no question of doctrine or principle need thereby be raised. But such is not the case at S. Agatha's. You do not ask for my sanction of the third altar on grounds of convenience (in the ordinary sense of the word); and, indeed, it is obvious that in that respect it would have no advantage over the second, or subsidiary, altar, to which I have raised no objection. You have explained to me that your wish for the addition rests, in the main, on quite different grounds. The altar in question is intended to have special association with a deceased friend, whose memory is rightly cherished in the parish.

"You desire that it should be surrounded with memorials of the dead, and that its special, though not exclusive, use should be for the celebration of what you describe as 'Mass for the Dead.'

"I endeavoured, in our recent conversation, to ascertain exactly what you mean by this term, and you explained candidly and clearly what it is that you believe and teach. You regard the Celebration of Holy Communion 'for the dead' as having the effect [you add, ' we know not how'] of shortening the period during which the souls of the faithful departed are in a state of 'purgation' or ' preparation,' and of hastening their admission to the Beatific state.

"Now, I have no wish to dictate to you, or to dogmatise, upon the mysterious and difficult question of what is known as 'prayer for the dead' - a term obviously capable of a great variety of meaning, ranging from the words we use in the Prayer for the Church Militant to doctrines of quite another sort. The whole subject is of great importance, and I will gladly discuss it with you hereafter; but, whatever liberty of private opinion and individual devotion may be permissible, I have no hesitation in saying that I should depart both from the spirit and the letter of our Church's formularies were I definitely to sanction the addition of a third altar to S. Agatha's with the knowledge that one main purpose of its erection is that it should be a centre for services and teaching of the character above described.

"I myself believe your teaching on this subject to be contrariant to some of the distinctive principles of the Church of England, and I am bound to add further that I am unable to reconcile your usages in celebrating the Holy Communion with the specific directions in the Book of Common Prayer, which both you and I have solemnly pledged ourselves to follow. You tell me, for example, that in S. Agatha's Church, where you have about twenty celebrations of the Holy Communion every week, more than half the celebrations on week-days, 'perhaps eight out of fifteen,' are in ordinary circumstances without communicants. You have so arranged that the celebrant shall know beforehand if any desire to communicate, and, if not, the celebrant omits the Exhortation, Confession, and Absolution from the Service.

"On week-days, unless they are festivals, the Creed and the Gloria in Excelsis are always omitted.

"It is impossible for me to disregard these facts in coming to a decision as to what I ought, at this juncture, to do. You have, as it seems to me, dealt practically at your will with our Church's Rules.

"I do not, for a moment, doubt that your motive is a good one. Your services are those which, in your individual opinion, are best calculated to lead your people into a knowledge of what you believe to be the truth.

"But the Church of England does not allow us thus to deal at our will with the Book of Common Prayer, and in the event of your deciding to remain at S. Agatha's, I must carefully discuss with you what modifications are required in order to bring your services into harmony with the Prayer Book.

"I need not repeat to you what I have so often said as to my sense of the value of your devoted work in the midst of special difficulties. Many of your distinctive Church Services seem to me to have a special value, as bringing home to the minds of unlearned people, by the use of anniversaries and memorials and otherwise, the links which bind us to the world unseen.

"These are, I believe, compatible with perfect loyalty to the Book of Common Prayer.

"I earnestly trust you may not think it necessary to sever yourself at present from a parish in which God has signally blessed your energy, your self-devotion, and your enthusiasm; and you may rely upon my constant endeavour to help and further your work in every legitimate way.

"I am, my dear Mr. Dolling,

"Yours very truly,

"RANDALL WINTON."

"WINCHESTER COLLEGE MISSION,
"LANDPORT, PORTSMOUTH,
9th December, 1895

"MY DEAR LORD BISHOP,

"I have to-day sent to Dr. Fearon my resignation. I think your account of our interviews is quite correct, except in one detail. I did not intend to say that I did not know how the Service of the Holy Communion affected the state of the dead. There is, however, one practical question.

"I must conduct the Services as I have for the last ten years. Do you wish me and my staff to go away at once, or to wait until Dr. Fearon has appointed my successor? I am ready to follow either course; only for fear of mistakes arising, I should like to say that as long as I am in charge the Sunday and daily services remain the same. I am, your lordship's obedient servant,

"R. R. DOLLING."

"FARNHAM CASTLE, SURREY,
"10th December, 1895.
"DEAR MR. DOLLING,

"I am exceedingly sorry to learn that you feel it to be your duty to leave St. Agatha's forthwith, but, of course, I recognise that your decision is perfectly consistent with what you said to me at our first interview.

"With regard to your question. What is to be done as to the services until your resignation takes effect, I have no sort of wish to press unfairly upon you, and I think it would be a grave misfortune were St. Agatha's Church to be closed pending the appointment of your successor.

"I think that until that appointment is made you had better continue to officiate. This will, I hope, be in accordance both with your own wish and with the wish of your people; and, though I must not be supposed to be giving formal sanction to the teaching or usages to which I have called your attention, and must adhere to my decision respecting the third altar, I am far from wishing to cause unnecessary difficulty in any way. Should anything lead you to modify your decision, and to desire to remain at St. Agatha's, it will be a pleasure to me to hear from you to that effect. I am glad that I succeeded in my endeavour to represent fairly what you told me at our interviews. The particular words to which alone you take exception in my account, are contained in the memorandum I made at the moment, and read to you for your approval. But the point is comparatively unimportant, and, of course, I accept the correction

you desire to make.
"I am, yours very truly,
"RANDALL WINTON."

"WINCHESTER COLLEGE MISSION, LANDPORT,
"11th December, 1895.
"DEAR LORD BISHOP,
"You will not blame me if I say that your letter amazes me. If my teaching is so contrary to the mind of the Church of England that it necessitates a step so disastrous as the disruption of a work like this, I cannot imagine how you can allow me to remain here one single day.

"I want, therefore, to make it clearly understood that I have unscreened the altar, and am using it, and that I shall conduct the services exactly as I have conducted them for the last eight years. I know you will understand that I do not say this in any spirit of bravado, but I desire, above all things, to be perfectly plain with you. Having said this, I am content to stay here for a short time, but there are two reasons that urge me to request you to fix a date not later than January 10th - (1) The Mission expenses are nearly £100 per month, and I am already very much overpressed with debts; in fact, winding up all the different charities and other expenses here, and repairing the parsonage and other property I have bought, and the paying for the church, will, I think, necessitate my begging £1500 before I leave, perhaps even more, and your action will very likely dry up some of our sources of charity. (2) I have to consider my own and my sister's health. I doubt if your lordship could imagine what it is to be here. It is almost impossible for us to go out of doors; the tears and lamentations of our poor people are more than we can bear for any length of time. I write this all with more confidence because your letter of today confirms my own remembrance of our interviews when I assured you I should have to leave, and, therefore, I am assured you have already considered the difficult question of a successor.

"I am, your lordship's obedient servant,
"R. R. DOLLING."

"OXFORD,
"13th December, 1895.
"DEAR MR. DOLLING,

"Owing to ceaseless pressure of other work I have not, since your letter reached me yesterday, had a free moment for writing to you.

"I can only repeat that I have no sort of wish to expedite the resignation on which you have, to my great regret, and in spite of my remonstrance, decided.

"I cannot easily reconcile your action in 'unscreening' the third altar with what you said to me on our first interview, but in present circumstances I say no more upon that, and I am anxious to make every allowance for your acts and words at a time of such stress and strain.

"I have just read in the *Times* what you are reported to have said at a meeting last night. I can hardly doubt that the report must be inaccurate. You could not, I feel sure, have represented me, after all that has passed, as thinking it 'necessary that disruption should take place,' or as harassing you with minute insistence on matters of mere rubrical detail. A grave question of Church order has come formally before me for decision as Bishop of the Diocese. With anxious care, and with an earnest wish to consider your difficulties, I have decided in accordance with what seems to be my duty, and thereupon, to my great regret, you have resigned at once, instead of waiting until the time you have publicly announced. I can scarcely conceive that anyone who studies our Ordinal, and realises a Bishop's obligations and responsibilities, could wish me to have acted otherwise than I have.

"I must in all kindness remonstrate against your resignation - even at a time of excitement - as though it were my act rather than your own. Few things in my life have caused me more sorrow and anxiety than this.

"With regard to the date when you cease to officiate at St. Agatha's; the appointment of your successor rests, as you know, with others, and not with me.

"I earnestly trust that if you persist in your resignation you will consider the difficulties of the Mission District, or Parish, and of

223

those with whom the appointment rests, and will do what you can to meet, or to relieve them.

"I am, yours very truly,

"RANDALL WINTON."

"WINCHESTER COLLEGE MISSION, LANDPORT,

"14th December, 1895.

"MY DEAR LORD BISHOP,

"I cannot quite understand what you mean by 'in spite of my remonstrance you are resigning.'

"Under your two predecessors we conducted service exactly as we desire to do in our new church. The little altar is the same, the memorials are the same, except that they are put on better materials. But no single act do we desire to perform, no single word to say, that was not done and said in old S. Agatha's. That is, as far as I can judge, if your predecessor had been here, we should not have gone away.

"He objected personally to the little altar, but not officially. The people here feel this so strongly that they want to lock up the new church and return to the old. Therefore it is surely through your action - unwilling action, I am sure - that I must either alter things or go away. Is there any other alternative? I cannot alter things, because I should be declaring to my own people that doctrines which have been taught among them for the last eight years I could conscientiously change at your bidding.

"I quite recognise your difficulty in the matter, and I hope that you will, in the enclosed paper, from which report that in the *Times* is condensed, read what I say about your action. It is your condemnation of my teachings, which you deem so erroneous and contrary to the forms of the Church of England, that necessitates the disruption.

"Dr. Fearon has already consulted with your Lordship about my successor; and has already, with your consent, offered the post to another man. So there is no difficulty about my going. Indeed he thinks the date - January 10 - reasonable. I have told him that I shall be delighted to show the new Priest the details of the work here, and introduce him to the church workers, etc.; and I have sent him a few statistics about the parish, copies of which I send to your Lordship,

and I am sure they will interest you. I am,
    "Your Lordship's obedient servant,
    "R. R. DOLLING."

                "FARNHAM CASTLE, SURREY,
                "17th December, 1895.
    "DEAR MR. DOLLING,
    "I thank you for your letter of the 14th. It followed me to
Bournemouth, where I was busy all day yesterday. Hence the delay in
my reply. The cutting you kindly sent me shows that, as I supposed,
the summary published in the London papers failed, perhaps
necessarily, to represent quite fairly what you really said; and I thank
you for the tone of many parts of your speech, and for the statistics
you have enclosed.

    "Pardon me if I say that it still seems to me to be true that 'you are
resigning in spite of my remonstrance.' When, at our first interview,
you told me of your intention, I deprecated it, and I do so still.
Elementary principles of Church order seem to me to suggest a
different course as at least possible, but I realise that you have made
up your mind, and that it is useless to press you further.

    "With regard to your reference to my predecessors in the See, you
cannot, I think, suppose that if the question which came formally
before me had come formally before either Bishop Thorold or Bishop
Harold Browne, the ultimate decision would have been a different
one.
    "I am, yours very truly,
    "RANDALL WINTON."

            "WINCHESTER COLLEGE MISSION, LANDPORT,
                "17th December, 1895.
    "MY DEAR LORD BISHOP,
    "The question would not have come before Dr. Thorold officially.
He provided for that by not requiring a new licence.

    "From memory I cannot speak with much authority of Bishop
Harold Browne's attitude towards us, except that several times
different Protestant Societies complained to him about us; and
though, as far as I remember, he wrote letters showing that he

personally did not approve of our methods, he never publicly or officially condemned them.

"But about Dr. Thorold I can speak with assurance. Directly he was designated by the Crown for the Bishopric, he asked me to stay with him in London, and we had two very long conversations about our work here; and I quite well remember his saying to me, when I told him how many celebrations we had on Sundays and on week-days, 'Surely it is not good for your people to go so often to Communion.' And when I explained to him that at some of the celebrations on Sundays, and many on week-days, there were no communicants, he turned round sharply, and said, 'Mr. Dolling, I do not like that at all.'

"After I had explained my difficulties to him, and the power that I believed these celebrations were to us and to my people, though I do not think he was convinced by my argument, he made no further objection.

"The first time he stayed here to confirm he went with me to look over the church. He was delighted with the memorials of the confirmed, &c.; but when he came to our little altar he said, 'I think that is the ugliest thing I ever saw.' And when I explained to him more about celebrations for the departed and prayers for the dead, he said, 'I don't believe in it for a moment.'

"We talked over the point for a long time, but I am positively sure that he never forbade me; and when I showed him at Farnham the plans of the new church, after he had said, 'I am so glad you are building a basilica,' though objecting to the baldacchino which was in the picture, I enlarged upon my intention of making the church as beautiful as I could by paintings, mosaics, &c. I said, 'We are going to have nothing ugly or unworthy in it; even the little altar which you thought so ugly the people have collected money to beautify, in memory of Ross' - and I told him the story. I think there were tears in his eyes when I had finished, and I am quite certain he said nothing.

"Of course I have written all this from memory, but I can give you an exact proof. Some years ago he was approached by the Protestant Alliance, on the subject of a book which our children used at their Celebration, and at his request, I withdrew it, and wrote a new book, which though he could not personally sanction, he permitted us to use. In the enclosed copy you will find in pages 25, 26, the words which the children use aloud directly after the Consecration, and especially on page 26, you will see the Memorial of the Dead. On pages 10-12 you will see what I teach about representing to the Eternal Father, both for the Living and the Dead, the Propitiatory Sacrifice, which our Lord made once for all upon the Cross.

"You will see, therefore, that he perfectly understood my attitude with regard to these two questions, and my method of teaching them to my children.

"If by going back to our old church, we could put back our altars in their former places, and be authorised by you to use the exact services we have used in the past under your predecessors, it might solve the difficulty.

"Or the alternative, whether in the new church at the High Altar or at the Subsidiary Altar, we could use the services we have used under your predecessor, is, I think, a question for your Lordship to suggest to me.

"But the two points which your letter seemed to forbid, were the offering of the Blessed Sacrifice for the Dead, and the Celebrations without Communion, and not the merely technical point whether there may be three altars in the church.

"Of course, Winchester is the chief factor in the question, and I think that the enclosed letter of Dr. Fearon, when I told him that our people had proposed, as a *modus vivendi*, that we should settle the question by going back into the old church, determines the matter as far as I am concerned. I am, your Lordship's obedient servant,

"R. RADCLIFFE DOLLING."

"FARNHAM CASTLE, SURREY,
"19th December, 1895.
"DEAR MR. DOLLING,

"I thank you for your letter of yesterday, telling me further details of what passed between my predecessors and yourself. What you say seems to make it quite clear that, whatever may have passed in conversation, the question now at issue was never formally submitted to either of them.

"My replies addressed yesterday to the two memorials from 'The

Church Workers of S. Agatha's' and from 'Communicants of S. Agatha's,' taken in connection with my previous letters to yourself, will, I hope, have made clear to you what is my position in the matter, and I do not think you will feel it to be necessary that I should add anything further. I am, yours very truly,
"RANDALL WINTON."

"WINCHESTER COLLEGE MISSION, LANDPORT,
"20th December, 1895.
"MY DEAR LORD BISHOP,
"I cannot bear to close this correspondence without saying that if, by any word of mine, I have spoken with disrespect either of you personally, or of your high office, I beg you will pardon it, and believe that it was perfectly unintentional.

"We leave on the morning of January 11th, and I shall be here every day till then getting matters finally arranged.

"I hardly like to suggest to your Lordship, because, of course, you know what is best; but I think it would materially help your guidance of this most needy place, in the future, if you could spare a few hours to see it before I go.

"There are matters about the church schools, which I won with great difficulty, which are especially pressing.

"I would offer to come to Farnham, if you would receive me, but I do not think you would be able to judge unless you came here.

"I am, your Lordship's obedient servant,
"R. R. DOLLING."

"Friday Night, 20th December, 1895,
"MY DEAR MR. DOLLING,
"In the stress of Ember days, with an ordination pending tomorrow, and some thirty men in the house, I can but send you a single line to reply to your letter just received. Pray believe that nothing could be further from my thoughts than to find cause of offence in any word you have said during this time of extreme trial for both of us. I have felt far too deeply for you to even think of such trifles. I remember you many times daily in my prayers.

"It can seldom, I hope, happen to anyone in a position of responsible authority in the Church to have to give a decision so painful to himself in the consequences it is found to involve, as that which it was my duty to give in this matter. I can but rest on the firm belief that He who calls one to the discharge of such responsibilities, will give ear to the prayer for grace that they may be discharged aright.

"While the question of what you would finally resolve to do remained in any way open, I felt that I might seriously confuse the issue to the minds of your people, were I to visit the parish, as though to judge of the work going on; whereas, as it seemed to me, the point at issue was quite independent of this. Now that you have come to a final decision, I should esteem it a privilege to go quietly and privately over the ground with you, and learn any details that you can tell me. Next week is not, perhaps, a good one for such a purpose, but it seems my only chance. If I go on Friday, 27th, would it suit you? I could be with you on that day from 11.39 to 2.15.

"I am, yours very truly,
"RANDALL WINTON."

Editor's Note

So ended the extraordinary work of Father Dolling in the rundown streets of Landport. Some commentators have said that with a little compromise on Father Dolling's part, he would have been allowed to stay on at his Landport mission, where he had made such a big difference to the lives of his parishioners. However, this is to misunderstand Father Dolling, a man who did what he believed to be right no matter what his critics said. He was thus replaced in 1896, just weeks after the new Saint Agatha's Church opened.

This left Father Dolling with a problem. He had raised most of the money for the building of the Church himself, but along with other expenses, had a shortfall of £3,090, an amount that he personally owed to his creditors. This is equivalent to approximately £365,000 in 2015.

Father Dolling set about paying back the money through sales of his book and through further fundraising. He did so with the same indefatigable energy he had applied whilst living in Portsmouth.

In 1897, Father Dolling toured the United States of America, where his preaching is said to have left a deep impression.

In 1898, he returned to the UK and received the living at Saint Saviour's Church, Poplar. This he retained until his death in 1902, at the age of 51.

Lightning Source UK Ltd.
Milton Keynes UK
UKOW05f1857180517
301516UK00015B/475/P